Betsy Sikora Siino

Alaskan Malamutes

Everything about Purchase, Care, Nutrition, Behavior, and Training

Filled with Full-color Photographs
Illustrations by Tana Hakanson

BARRON'S

2 CONTENTS

INTRODUCING THE ALASKAN MALAMUTE

An infectious smile, a courageous heart, and an indomitable spirit mark the Alaskan malamute as a treasure to everyone—well, almost everyone.

Northern Light— The Alaskan Malamute

Why, some among us might wonder, would anyone be interested in a dog that may not sit when you ask him to sit, has much difficulty walking at the heel, and seems conveniently to forget all he has been taught (or to develop an unexplained temporary loss of hearing) at the most inopportune moments? Aren't dogs meant to strive for obedience, to do our every bidding, and to sit anxiously at our feet awaiting our next command? Some dogs are, perhaps, but not the Alaskan Malamute.

What this dog's critics do not realize—and despite the animal's breathtaking beauty and infectious grin, it does have his critics—is that the Malamute is always listening. He receives

For centuries, Alaskan Malamutes have shared a deep affection for, and partnership with, humans.

and understands every word we say, every subtle gesture we make. He just seems to consider himself above all that dog obedience business, viewing himself instead as an equal partner with the humans in his life. It would seem he has deserved such a distinction.

For thousands of years, the Alaskan Malamute has stood prominently on equal footing with humans. He learned very early in his evolution that his reason for being was to use his brain, wit, and canine sixth sense to protect those odd two-legged creatures for whom he had developed quite a legendary affection. He succeeded magnificently in this mission, saving the lives of countless Arctic natives and newcomers alike, who would have met rather untimely, not to mention uncomfortable, ends in the permafrost. If contemporary Malamutes thus decide, on occasion, that they do not care to sit or fetch a ball, perhaps it is because they have concerns of greater import on their minds.

The Alaskan Malamute is named for the Mahlemut people of Alaska's Kotzebue Sound.

There is a lovely scene in the classic Disney film *The Lion King,* when young Simba learns from his father that the stars in the sky are the spirits of the kings that came before, and that they are always there to guide and protect the mortals still bound to the earth. During those inevitable moments when it appears that the Malamute, ever dignified in his demeanor, has been transported to another world, think of that scene. Imagine that as the dog looks off into the distance, perhaps ignoring a *down* command, he is communing with all the Malamutes that came before, their spirits manifested not in the stars but in the northern lights. Perhaps theirs are the voices that guide this dog across the ice and bolster his value system that to this day embodies a profound love of the human species. If I were stranded in the Arctic, I would take great comfort in knowing a Malamute, and all the Malamutes that came before, were by my side.

An Ancient Past

We call it the last frontier, the land of the midnight sun. But to those who know and love dogs, Alaska is much more than a vast, frozen wilderness that sits at the top of the world—it is home to the magnificent Alaskan Malamute.

The true beginnings of this dog will always remain a mystery. All we are privileged to know is that the earliest ancestors of all of the great northern dog breeds lived among early representatives of our own species for thousands of years. Because of the interdependent relationship they have for so long enjoyed with our species, they were probably some of the first dogs to have been domesticated.

In light of so rich a heritage, the Malamute is believed to have bred true for centuries, if not millennia, sculpted in the biological tradition of evolution by its Arctic homeland and the people who carved out a living there.

Hailing from the Kotzebue Sound on Alaska's northwest coast, the Malamute takes his name from the native Eskimos, or Inuits, who resided there known as the Mahlemuts. Living as they did in a land of very little vegetation and frigid temperatures, these people depended on dogs for their very survival. The Mahlemuts relied on dogs not only as partners for hunting large game that was more often than not located far from home, but also, once successful in their mission, to haul that large game home over vast expanses of frozen tundra. The dogs that could fulfill this double duty had to be powerful and muscular with impeccable instincts, stamina, and endurance, attributes far more critical than speed.

Blessed as they were with these quintessential freighting dogs, the Mahlemut people did not require large teams of dogs to meet the challenges of their daily lives—yet another gift Malamutes brought to their namesake humans. The Malamutes provided more muscle per dog, and their efficient metabolisms required less fuel than one would expect from so large an animal.

The Malamute Heart

Beyond simply taking the name of their human family, Alaska's Malamutes became intertwined with the people with whom they shared their lives. The dogs and their humans evolved together, through the centuries taking on similar characteristics that enhanced the interdependence upon which their mutual survival relied.

Examples of this phenomenon existed in every aspect of the Mahlemuts' lives. Out of necessity, for example, the Mahlemut people were tireless workers. The greatest insult they could level against one of their dogs was to expect it to sit idle—or, worse yet, to leave it at home when it came time to embark on a hunt. The Mahlemuts knew that their survival required cooperation and teamwork. Their dogs, though they could be predatory and argumentative, also understood that all must work together for the survival of both the canine and human members of the team. The Mahlemuts were strong and independent and so, of course, were their dogs. Out on the ice, the people, in fact, trusted their dogs' instincts over their

Hailing as he does from the Arctic, an Alaskan Malamute can withstand the frigid temperatures found at the top of the world.

own, thus placing their very lives in the care of their animals.

Even on a more benign plane, the people and their dogs mirrored one another, especially where children were concerned. The Mahlemuts loved children and treated them with kindness and respect. Their dogs bonded with the young of the village, too, thus spawning a legendary love for children that remains one of the breed's most outstanding characteristics today.

From work to play to the way in which they viewed the world, the Mahlemut people could not have survived without their dogs, who not only made their peoples' daily lives possible, but no doubt brightened each day as well.

Dog of Legend and Lore

That the Mahlemut people treasured their dogs goes without saying. But while many treated their Malamutes almost as family members, life was harsh for humans and dogs in those Arctic settlements. Both dogs and humans had to deal with the often cruel realities of their everyday existence. When food was scarce, the dogs suffered right along with their people, and, at the mercy as they were of treacherous climate and terrain, when dogs misbehaved or failed to hold up their end of the work, they were rarely given a second chance to correct their ways.

Nevertheless, the bond that existed between the Mahlemuts and their dogs was unique, and the esteem with which the people held their canine partners was genuine. This fact did not escape the notice of the first explorers who ventured into this frozen, long unknown corner of the world in the 1800s. Upon their arrival, these adventurers invariably sang the praises of the dogs that were not only partners in survival, but pets as well.

The dogs were subsequently immortalized in the journals kept by these newcomers, who could not resist the beauty of the animals, the warmth of their personalities, and the bond they shared with their caretakers. While indeed the dogs of the frozen north, whether Malamute, Siberian husky, or Samoyed, had to be tough, with few exceptions they were also infinitely loyal to the humans in their lives. The immortality these northern dogs found in those early writings was only the beginning.

Enter the Outsiders

The trickle of explorers that came to Alaska throughout the 1800s became a flood with the discovery of gold there in 1896. As happens whenever that magical word "gold" is uttered, Alaska and the Yukon were inundated by people in search of wealth, many of them spurred on by legends of fist-sized nuggets lying on the beaches and by the romantic tales of Jack London.

London is often credited with drawing the world's attention, not only to the adventures of life in Alaska, but also to the dogs that inhabited that frozen world. While his dogs and their often vicious behavior tended to be products of the author's imagination, he vividly illuminated the bond between Alaska's dogs and their men, and the world could not help but listen.

What rang most true in London's writings was the transition that was occurring at the time of the gold rush in Alaska's canine culture. Here lived a unique collection of dogs that for centuries had been bred and raised to pull sleds across the frozen tundra, and to live their lives in symbiotic cohabitation with those few humans who were either born to life at the top of the world, or were called there in search of gold, independence, or freedom from the law.

While most prospectors sought the services of freighting dogs (a calling to which the Malamute was historically suited), and many began to fill their idle hours pitting their dogs against each other in weight-pulling contests (another natural Malamute calling), it was the racing of the dogs that drew the most enthusiastic following.

While the Malamute had handily earned the title of Alaska's premier freighting dog, the vocation of dog racing was better suited for smaller, lighter dogs that could reach and sustain greater speeds than the large Malamute was capable of. Consequently, the Malamute's bloodlines, along with others, were used for the development of what would become the favored racers: the Siberian husky and the Alaskan husky. Because of similarities in markings, the Malamute is often mistaken for the smaller, lightweight, even delicate, Siberian. With a broader head, at least double the size, and a calmer temperament than his Siberian counterpart, the Malamute has remained a better freighter than a racer.

In the Line of Duty

As the twentieth century progressed, word of the Malamute's indomitable strength, stamina, courage, and heart reached those who were organizing Admiral Richard E. Byrd's expeditions to the South Pole. Among the dogs recruited for the two journeys to the bottom of the world were Malamutes, many of which ultimately suffered injury and illness and met cruel ends. Yet the successful exploration of this vast continent could not have been accomplished without the dogs.

The same can be said for the Malamute's contribution to America's efforts in World War II. Having already proven their mettle in Alaska and the South Pole, Malamutes were next recruited to serve as army dogs during the war.

Because of their natural talents, Malamutes were used to pull sleds in snow-covered areas that were inaccessible to other, more mechanical means of transportation. They were similarly used as pack animals to carry weaponry and ammunition across the frozen ground, and they served as search-and-rescue dogs, a task made possible by their ancient abilities to navigate endless fields of ice and snow. Again, many of the dogs perished in the line of duty, a sad fate to which the Malamute had long been accustomed.

Official Recognition

No longer shrouded in Alaska's ice and snow, after the turn of the century the reputation of the Alaskan Malamute spread south to people with more recreational goals in mind. Particularly interested in this dynamic dog were canine devotees in New England who were just beginning to embrace the new sport of sled dog racing. In the

Malamutes have captured the hearts of people seeking both work ethic and family loyalty in a canine companion.

course of their discovery, several of these people found themselves enamored of the Malamute.

The breed was not in good shape at the time. The crossbreeding of Malamutes in Alaska with such breeds as Saint Bernards and similar giants, due to the lack of enough native dogs to meet the demands of the gold hunters seeking large freighting dogs, led to a severe decline in the pure Malamute population and an all-around degeneration during the gold rush of the ancient gene pool. This situation was rectified in time, however, by those fledgling breeders in the lower forty-eight who took it upon themselves to ensure that the Malamute would be preserved and remain pure for all time. Their success in this mission ultimately led to the official recognition of the Alaskan Malamute by the American Kennel Club in 1935.

Wolf/Dog Hybrids: A Special Problem

While irresponsible breeding can harm every breed of dog, it presents a special problem to the world of Alaskan Malamutes: the problem of wolf/dog hybrids.

Just as Malamutes are frequently mistaken for wolves, so have they emerged as the "ideal" cross in misguided attempts to create a wolf with the temperament of a dog. The offspring of such crossings tend to be unstable, usually mistreated animals that end up with status-seeking individuals who are unable to care for an animal of wolf breeding. Wolf/dog hybrids are typically large, powerful animals with a special affinity for destroying furniture, land-scaping, and architecture; and far too many children have fallen victim to the animals' predatory reflexes. Most are virtually untrain-able and cannot be housebroken. They are con-fused animals of both wild and domestic blood, and thus their temperaments may never be considered completely reliable.

Once the misguided individuals who take these animals as pets recognize their grave error—realizing that no, this animal cannot reside in a two-bedroom urban condominium or be allowed anywhere near the family's four-year-old child—it is too late. The animal ends up the victim, perhaps beaten or imprisoned by the owner, abandoned on a country road or busy highway, or, if fortunate, relegated to one of the nations' overcrowded animal shelters. In most cases, the most humane fate for such animals is euthanasia. It is doubtful that most could ever be rehabilitated, and very few indi-viduals know how to care properly for these animals. In addition, animal shelters can ill-afford the financial hit when a court rules that a shelter is responsible for adopting out a hybrid that ultimately attacks a child.

So prevalent did the problem of wolf/dog hybrids become in the 1990s, that communi-ties nationwide banned the ownership of the animals, a trend that would ultimately do great harm to the Alaskan Malamute. Forbidden to keep hybrids, owners would simply license their hybrids as Malamutes. When hybrids bite, then, as many do, the attacks are attributed to Malamutes, causing an unjust inflation of the bite statistics for this breed. Many Malamute enthusiasts have regarded this situation as a terrible threat to their breed, which is increas-ingly being labeled a biting breed. This in turn leads to a denial of insurance coverage and even banishment from some communities—in part because their bloodlines have been diluted by the blood of animals that are not even of the Malamute's own species.

The bottom line: Avoid any temptation to cross your Malamute with a wolf or to permit others to do so. You may encounter unethical breeders promising large puppy profits, but they neglect to mention that most people who buy these animals abandon them before they reach two years of age, or that liability judgments against owners whose wolf/dog hybrids attack children (the most common victims) can bank-rupt a family. Anyone breeding Malamutes should breed their dogs only with pure Mala-mutes. Only in this way can breeders pay proper tribute to the great heritage of the Alaskan Malamute, a breed that does not deserve to be degraded by a fad or get-rich-quick schemes.

It's no wonder that generations of Malamutes have so successfully charmed and inspired the human species.

The Modern Malamute

Where legends are concerned, none is more prevalent in the story of the Malamute than the belief that this dog simply must be part wolf, a legend that reached a fever pitch during the gold rush days. How else, ask those who continue to embrace this notion, could this dog have developed such a wolflike appearance? Yet, despite the commonly held belief that the Mahlemuts would tether a bitch to a pole in the snow so she could be bred by a wolf, countless historians, and the Mahlemut people themselves, insist the Malamute is pure domestic dog, no closer genetically than any other dog to the lupine branch of the canine family.

Get to know today's Malamute, and the obvious differences between him and the wolf are clear. While some similarities exist, such as that breathtakingly beautiful physique, a tendency to howl, and a lack of talent as a watchdog, the Malamute, unlike the wolf, has lived intimately with humans for thousands of years, evident today in the unique affection he harbors for the human species.

Today's Malamute carries on the heritage of his predecessors. He continues to revel in the family pack, to crave human companionship, and to enjoy a special affinity for children. He continues to excel as a sled dog, thriving when the thermometer's mercury drops below the freezing point, and even competing in weight-pulling competitions when the opportunity arises. And he continues to seek adventure in his daily life.

Success in a partnership with a Malamute, therefore, requires an owner who is willing to learn the Malamute's story and to respect the significance of it. The modern Malamute must be viewed in light of the ancient Malamute—the two cannot be separated. An individual willing to make this effort, one who shares the same wild and adventurous spirit of this ancient breed, is the individual with whom the Malamute will be most comfortable—and the individual who will be most content living with this magnificent animal.

BIG DOG,
BIG DECISION

Those who consider a Malamute companion are wise to think long and hard—and realistically— before taking such a dog into their homes and hearts.

A Malamute in the House

The Alaskan Malamute, for obvious reasons, appeals to those attracted to the majestic countenance of the wolf. Resembling that wild creature as closely as she does, the Malamute brings the ancient spirit of the North into the daily lives of mere mortals who don't happen to reside in the last frontier.

The popular media has enthusiastically embraced the Malamute's wolflike image, casting Malamutes as body doubles for their wild cousins. This, however, often results in a negative public response not only to the "vicious" man-eating wolf the Malamute is asked to impersonate, but also to the Malamute herself, which is then mistaken by those ignorant of such matters as a vicious wolflike dog on city streets. This has

Malamutes require owners who are properly prepared for such large and demanding dogs.

occurred repeatedly in preposterous scenes in movies and television shows, in which packs of smiling Malamutes, their lush, curled tails wagging in unison, "threaten" to devour lost hikers or various and sundry action heroes.

Though such media imagery has caused some to fear the Malamute, others can think of no finer pet than this beautiful, rather challenging beast with the look of the wolf and the ancient soul of the Arctic.

Given the Malamute's rich and rather arduous past, it is remarkable that the breed has remained pure. Although she is probably larger today, the Malamute probably still resembles very closely the original Malamutes of the Arctic. Then as now, the Malamute continues to grace the homes in which she resides with the gifts she has acquired through thousands of years of living with humans, attributes that can be traced to a life as companion, lifeline, and soulmate. Only those who appreciate this heritage should dare to invite this unique animal into their homes.

Are You the Right Owner for a Malamute?

Malamutes demand much from their owners. They demand to occupy prominent positions in their family packs; they demand to play central roles in every family activity; and they demand that their instincts, body language, and vocalizations be respected and, when appropriate, heeded. In exchange, they willingly return tenfold to the worthy owner what is given to them.

Yet that owner cannot be a run-of-the-mill individual. This individual, like the Malamute herself, must possess an adventurous, yet sensitive heart. This does not mean he or she must take daily forays out on to the glacier, but each day must be ripe with some sort of activity in which the dog, too, can participate.

Also critical to the relationship is the understanding that Malamutes possess an acute sensitivity to all the goings-on in their households and to the dynamics between family members. They react instinctively to the most subtle body positions and vocal inflections, especially during arguments and moments of strife, and they expect their owners to be just as sensitive toward them.

Learning to Speak Canine

The worthy Malamute owner should learn all he or she can from books, trainers, behaviorists, and from experience with the dog herself, about canine language. One of the greatest insults to the Malamute is an owner who does not try to communicate succinctly with his or her dog. For thousands of years this animal has lived among people who offered her that respect inherent to their mutual communication. To do otherwise could mean death to both the people and the dogs, when, say, the musher guiding the sled failed to heed the lead dog's warning of a crevasse in the ice or some other pending danger of which the dog's sixth sense warned.

This type of relationship is what the Malamute continues to expect from those humans she calls family. As the relationship blossoms, owners begin to take for granted the fact that the dog seems practically able to read their minds, to respond to their human thoughts even before they have dared to acknowledge them themselves.

Given the breed's history, it should come as no surprise that the Malamute is considered one of the canine family's most people-loving members. And the dog rarely discriminates in this mission. Although her size, as well as her wolflike appearance, will surely keep disreputable types at bay, most owners learn quickly that their beloved pet will gladly welcome strangers into their homes and probably lead them right to the valuables while they're at it!

While a young Malamute puppy may be irresistible, it will someday grow into a very large dog in need of an owner dedicated to discipline and consistency.

Who's the Boss?

Malamute owners also learn very quickly that the breed is one of the strongest willed and most independent members of the canine family tree. Without these attributes, the dogs would have perished on the ice, never surviving to see the twenty-first century. But they did survive, as did their independent natures. As a result, they require owners who are more than just patient, but accepting, as well. Nevertheless, it is critical from the very beginning that the dog learn that she is not the boss.

This does not mean it should be beaten into submission or otherwise mistreated. Rather, the best way to convince this pack-sensitive dog that she is subordinate is through such subtle tactics as assigning her a spot other than your bed as her sleeping place and insisting, with firmness and consistency, that she obey your commands every time without fail. She need not perform the perfect *sit* or *heel,* but she must understand that you mean business. You can help get this message across to the dog most effectively during puppyhood, when you must resist the desire to overindulge the adorable youngster. Spoil the pup, and you will end up with a demanding, potentially aggressive 100-plus-pound (45.4 kg) dog that is suddenly deaf in both ears whenever you issue a command.

The Malamute's independent nature is often mistaken for a lack of intelligence, often by trainers who are more accustomed to working with the likes of willing Golden Retrievers. While "stubborn" may be a valid label for this dog, veteran Malamute keepers would never accuse their breed of a lack of intelligence. You simply have to make the lessons interesting, that's all. The trick is to convince the dog that there is a good reason for her to do what you are asking.

Daily walks and exercise are a must.

Never underestimate this animal's understanding of what you are teaching her. Assuming you are clear and consistent with your instructions, it's a safe bet your dog will understand quickly. Whether or not she will deign to obey, however, is another story, as she may choose instead to test the intensity of your resolve.

Keeping Your Malamute Busy

Boredom and Malamutes don't mix. This dog is generally happiest learning more complex, purposeful skills, say, those required to pull a sled through a blizzard or to accompany an owner on cross-country skis. In other words, this dog must be kept busy, both physically and mentally, or those abundant energies may just have to be vented in more destructive directions—perhaps in tearing apart the living room furniture or digging trenches in the backyard. A dog of this size and strength can do quite a lot of damage when she sets her mind to it.

An Owner's Resumé

Put yourself in the Malamute's place. Given her ancestral heritage, how do you measure up to the individual she would choose, if she could choose, as her owner? Living with a Malamute is dramatically different from living with most other breeds of dog, so before you take that plunge and decide to buy a Malamute, evaluate your Malamute-ownership resumé from the dog's point of view:

Where do you live? Yes, the ideal domicile for a Malamute is a house with a large properly fenced (six-foot minimum) yard, but this is not to say that the dog must be simply banished to life outdoors never to set foot in the house. Inherent in this breed's love of people is the need to share its people's lives fully. Malamutes do enjoy and require ample time outdoors, but they also relish the opportunity to spend the evening by the fire in the company of family. The Malamute can reside in a more cramped dwelling, even one without large acreage surrounding it, but only if she is offered a great deal of exercise and mental stimulation every

single day—a requirement true of any Malamute in any living situation.

What is your dog experience? If they had their "druthers," Malamute rescuers and reputable breeders would prefer that only those with experience with dogs—especially experience with large, headstrong dogs—take the step into the adventure that is the Alaskan Malamute. Newcomers can succeed, but they must be willing to do their homework and find mentors who can help them along.

What are your expectations? Before you even begin contemplating the prospect of living with a Malamute, you must honestly evaluate the reality of living with a savvy, strong-willed dog that can ultimately weigh as much as 100, 110, even 120 pounds (45.4, 49.9, 54 kg). Do you have the time, inclination, and physical and temperamental ability required to mold the behavior of so complex, even dominant, an animal in positive directions? Do you truly want a dog that demands to be an integral part of every project, every activity? Are you active enough for a partnership with a Malamute? This isn't an exercise machine you purchase with grand resolutions to "get in shape," only to cast it away in a corner once the novelty and your commitment wane.

Pay attention to more practical concerns, as well:

• Will a full-grown Malamute fit in your car?
• Are there other pets in the household that may inspire predatory impulses in this dog?
• Do you mind having hair all over the furniture, in the carpet, on your clothes and in your food? If so, perhaps a Nordic dog of any breed is not appropriate for your household.

To keep your Malamute happy, keep her busy.

What about the rest of the family? If there are children in the family, that will certainly please the resident Malamute, but the kids and dog must be monitored to prevent any unforeseen mishaps that can occur between a young child and a very large dog. As for the young Malamute, everyone must be warned that she will not remain the roly-poly teddy-bear-like puppy for long. Are all in the family willing to commit to this soon-to-be-large and potentially domineering dog's training and socialization, to practice consistency, and to refuse to allow the pup to engage in behaviors that will be forbidden once the dog is grown?

Can you afford a Malamute? The proper care of any dog can be costly, what with veterinary care, kenneling, equipment, food, etc., but a Malamute, for obvious reasons, is particularly costly to feed, house, board, and transport.

Another expense associated with Malamute keeping is that of the time involved. In addition to the time required for daily exercise and activity, you may need to divide your dog's daily food rations into two or three small meals a day to keep the dog more comfortable and to prevent the deadly condition of canine bloat (see page 72). Also time consuming can be the grooming of this dog, which requires regular and very thorough brushing, especially when the coat is shedding.

Can you offer a lifetime commitment? You don't have to be born with a natural sensitivity to and understanding of the nuances of Malamute communication, but the successful human partner of this dog will exhibit a genuine desire to master these skills. You must commit not only to the dog, but to your own patience and sensitivity. Work with a trainer who understands the unique Malamute character, and who respects the breed's intelligence and the fascinating ways in which her mind works.

In reviewing your qualifications as a prospective Malamute owner, ask yourself and your family the proper questions and be honest with the answers. Assure yourself and your family that your desire for this breed runs far deeper than simply wishing for a beautiful dog that many will mistake for a wolf. Success is greatest for those who feel a true kinship with this animal and see that as their motivation for living with one.

The Ideal Malamute

Next on the agenda is to become familiar with the American Kennel Club breed standard for the Malamute, a tool that will come in handy as you begin your search for a new Malamute family member. Armed with this information, you will be prepared to evaluate the potential candidates and make the best choice possible.

The standard exists as a model for breeders, offering them an ideal to strive for in their breeding programs. The overriding goal is to keep the breed pure and breeding true. While every AKC breed has a standard, the Malamute, as a member of the AKC Working Group, is bred according to a standard in which form follows function. Bred to work, Malamutes are judged in the show ring for their potential as working sledge dogs, and their conformation must lend itself to that purpose.

General Appearance

The Malamute should present a strong, dignified, powerful picture of a dog with a deep chest, a straight back, and a lushly furred curled tail that the dog carries proudly over her back.

Engineered for pulling sleds and sledges over treacherous terrain, the Malamute's legs should be large boned and well muscled, coupled with equally large feet with thick pads insulated by a dense growth of hair. Atop her wide, thickly muzzled head, her erect, wedge-shaped ears remain alert to the most subtle of sounds. The dog's noble, often serenely intelligent gaze emanates from almond-shaped eyes, which should be brown (blue eyes, acceptable in Siberian huskies, are a disqualifying fault in Malamutes).

Size

While Malamutes are found in a range of sizes, the average male, as reflected in the standard, stands about 25 inches (63.5 cm) at the shoulder and weighs in at approximately 85 pounds (38.6 kg); the female is slightly smaller, standing approximately 23 inches (58 cm) at the shoulder and weighing in at 75 pounds (34 kg). Many Malamutes are much larger than this, however, and, assuming they are physically proportioned and sport the correct movement and structure, the larger dogs are rarely penalized in the show ring. There is danger, however, in modern trends that encourage the breeding of giant Malamutes—dogs that can reach as much as 150 pounds (68 kg). Such excess size and weight can stress the dog's muscles and bones, and theories suggest that they may stress the heart, as well.

Color

The typical Malamute is usually gray in color, ranging from a very light gray to black, with white undersides, although pure white and a rare red variation with lighter eyes is also acceptable. The dog's coat color is usually complemented by either a mask of color across the dog's white face or a cap of color at the top of her head, markings that, despite all-around similarities in color, differentiate this dog clearly from a wolf.

Coat

Like all members of the Nordic family of dogs, the Malamute sports a thick double coat, consisting of a soft, woolly undercoat that acts as an insulator, combined with a longer, rather coarse coat of guard hairs that stand out from the dog's body. This ingenious system protects the dog in those legendary sub-zero temperatures of her homeland, yet with ample shade and constant access to fresh cool water, today's pet Malamute should fare well in warmer climes, as well. When temperatures are extreme, such as 100°F (37.8°C) and above, the dog should be kept indoors during the day and exercised only when the heat subsides. Her owner should also resist the temptation to shave the coat. Veteran owners cringe at the thought, knowing that Malamutes do not adjust well emotionally to the removal of one of their primary physical characteristics.

Temperament

The standard addresses the Malamute's temperament as well. In keeping with the dog's ancient past, today's Malamute is described in her breed standard as loyal, affectionate, friendly, dignified, and devoted. With this standard guiding its breeding, it is little wonder that the well-bred Malamute commands such enthusiasm from her human companions.

Adult or Puppy?

Once you have come to understand the mechanics of evaluating Malamutes effectively, you must decide just what kind of Malamute you want—an adult or a puppy.

Each has benefits and each has drawbacks. While many people dream of bringing a new puppy into the house and raising her into the lovely adult it is destined to be, doing this right requires a great deal of time and effort.

To raise a puppy correctly, you must, for all practical purposes, become the young dog's surrogate mom and commit to molding the youngster into a well-behaved adult. This, as any mom can testify, can be a full-time job. Obedience training, household manners, house-training, and socialization are the ingredients that lead to a well-behaved adult Malamute. Such a dog does not occur as a natural phenomenon; she is the product of hours of nurturing, sweat, and consistency.

Those who honestly do not believe they have the time to raise a puppy, but believe they must have a Malamute in the house, may be more interested in adopting an older dog that has already received her basic education and experienced the challenging impulses of puppy adolescence. In fact, many have found they prefer a dog that is five or six years of age, as this dog will tend to be more settled, her youthful exuberance will have mellowed somewhat, and she will be more content devoting her time to her duties as family companion. If you overcome the prejudice too many people harbor against bringing an older dog into the home, you may just find a treasure.

Launching the Treasure Hunt

Once upon a time, Alaskan Malamutes could be found only in Alaska. Today, fortunately for those who seek to live with one of these dogs, you may find fine specimens without making a pilgrimage to the land of the midnight sun.

To help ensure a successful match, choose your new pet with your head as well as your heart.

The Breeder

Should you decide that you would like to purchase an Alaskan Malamute from a breeder, which many consider the ideal source for a purebred puppy, you will need to be prepared not only to choose the right puppy or dog, but also the right breeder. The best way to do this is to contact several, and find out how they operate.

In the purest sense, the reputable, ethical breeder breeds not for profit, but out of a true devotion to a breed. Such breeders are well aware of the genetic problems inherent in their breed and do all they can to prevent them in their lines. They take a great deal of care in placing their puppies in good homes, interviewing buyers extensively and turning down anyone who doesn't seem up to their standards. Their dogs can be expensive, but in most cases, you are getting what you pay for.

The best breeders will guarantee their dogs against genetic problems, will offer a full refund if such problems arise, and will agree in writing to take their dogs back in the future at any time, for any reason. In working with such a breeder, you may find a variety of dogs available. You may place your name on a waiting list for a young puppy, or decide that a retired show or sled Malamute is more appropriate for your lifestyle. The key is to be patient.

What too many potential buyers mistakenly believe is that breeders produce only show dogs. In fact, most puppies in a particular litter will be of pet quality. Given the value of a precious family pet, this simply means that the pet-quality puppy deviates in often subtle ways from the breed standard, but borne of the same bloodlines and diligence that begets the show champion, that pet-quality pup radiates with the same health and vitality.

When meeting with a breeder of such animals, evaluate the overall breeding operation:
✔ Is the facility clean?
✔ Do the dogs look healthy, friendly, and well cared for?
✔ Is the breeder knowledgeable about both the breed and his or her dogs?
✔ Does the breeder seem committed more to the dogs or to potential profits?
✔ Does the breeder guarantee his or her stock?

The ethical breeder will question the prospective buyer just as extensively as the buyer questions the breeder to ensure that the puppies will find a proper and permanent home. This breeder will also conduct the sale via contract (a breeder without a contract should be avoided), and a commitment to the Malamute Club's Code of Ethics will be reflected in that contract.

The Contract: Such a contract is beneficial to all parties involved: buyer, breeder, and dog. It protects the new owner by guaranteeing the genetic health of the dog and her parents; it demands contractually that pet animals be spayed or neutered (a provision backed up by the AKC's Limited Registration, which will not issue regular registration papers to a dog officially designated as a pet by its breeder); and it will allow the owner to return the dog if he or she can no longer keep the animal in the future. Such guarantees, combined with healthy, well-bred Malamutes from which to choose, add up to a successful breeder/buyer transaction, and a long-term Malamute/owner relationship.

The Animal Shelter

What many prospective dog owners do not realize is that the nation's animal shelters are filled not only with mixed-breed dogs, but with purebreds as well. Even the friendly, majestic Malamute is often found awaiting a new home from behind the chain link of an animal shelter, typically the victim of an owner who was ill-prepared to care for and work with such a dog.

If you find a Malamute in a shelter, she will most likely be an older adolescent puppy or a mature adult, cast aside by people who adored the dog when she was a puppy that resembled a young wolf, but whose interest waned when

Finding the Perfect Breeder

Finding a breeder of healthy, well-adjusted Alaskan Malamutes is serious business, but there are plenty of resources available. First, tap in to the local dog network in your area: veterinarians, groomers, boarding kennels, and animal shelters. Let them know what you are looking for, and you may just find the same names pop up again and again (a good sign).

Dog shows are another excellent source. Here, with dog people congregated in one location, you can speak with breeders and see their dogs. The American Kennel Club can provide you with information on the shows in your region. You can also contact the Alaskan Malamute Club of America (see contact information at the end of this book), which can direct you to member breeders throughout the country, as well as rescue networks, should you be interested in adopting a rescue dog. And finally, there is the Internet, which has made locating breeders easier than it ever was before. Be warned, however, that a slick website does not guarantee the quality or ethics of the breeder behind it.

confronting the monumental commitment of caring for the full-grown Malamute. Do not let this situation discourage you. With the proper commitment from her owner, this dog, too, can become a fine pet.

The adopted shelter Malamute will probably be in need of some rehabilitation, best pursued with the help of a canine behaviorist well versed in both Malamute character and in the special needs of the adopted shelter dog. While this Malamute may be headstrong and lacking in the early socialization that is best conducted during puppyhood, the natural people-loving nature of this breed will help her to fit readily into the family, inspiring all to face the challenge of adjustment and training with enthusiasm.

The Breed Rescue Organization

While there will always be Malamutes that fail to be rescued, the Alaskan Malamute Assistance League, a national network that works with Malamute rescue groups across the nation, tracks available dogs and sets standard policies on how they should be fostered and adopted. While the League cannot save them all, its goal is to keep the number of homeless, unwanted Malamutes to a minimum. Rescue is carried out by volunteers who take the dogs in from private owners and shelters, and then match them up with new owners who will offer them a second chance at the life and commitment they deserve.

As with shelter dogs, rescue dogs are typically older. In working with a good rescue group, prospective owners are carefully screened for their fitness for life with a Malamute. Rescue dogs, in turn, are ideally kept in foster homes, where rescue volunteers can get to know the dogs' quirks, and work to correct problems, thus easing the dogs' transitions into their new homes.

Selecting a Healthy Malamute Pet

The most valuable tool available to the potential Malamute buyer is the Code of Ethics issued by the Alaskan Malamute Club of Amer-

While black and shades of gray with white are the most common and traditional Malamute colors, a rare red variation with lighter eyes is also acceptable.

ica, the breed's national club. While there are no guarantees, a dog bred according to the tenets of the code has every chance of being the pet you dream of.

Within the code are stipulations that forbid breeders from selling puppies to entities for the breeding of wolf/dog hybrids. It addresses the genetic problems that affect Malamutes, emphasizes the need for spay/neuter contracts for non-show dogs, and states that breeders will be responsible for the dogs they produce for the lifetime of those dogs. The code, therefore, offers potential buyers a context for evaluating potential pets, as this is a choice that must be made with the mind rather than the heart.

For this critical evaluation process, several factors come into play. Male Malamutes, for example, may be larger and more domineering than their female counterparts, and puppies may be more difficult to evaluate objectively because of the "cuteness" factor. While the significance of such elements will vary depending on whether you are buying a show puppy or adopting a rescue dog, it is best to be as informed as possible about the breed and thus about the dogs you will be meeting.

Meeting Mom and Dad

Temperament, health, and conformation can all be passed on from one generation to the next, so meeting Mom and Dad can help you evaluate certain characteristics inherent in a particular Malamute family.

Meeting Mom is especially critical, because the quality of her maternal instincts can have long-term effects on how the puppy interacts with people and other dogs. Steer clear of puppies from a shy, timid, and/or aggressive dam, as her behavior may be passed on both genetically and by example to her offspring, even if she is with them for only the first eight weeks of life.

A friendly, nurturing mom, on the other hand, who is attentive to her young family and affectionate toward the humans in her life, will offer even very young puppies a positive role model whose early care will leave an indelible imprint on her puppies' adult behavior.

The Genetic Blueprint

The Alaskan Malamute, like virtually every breed of dog, is prone to several genetic conditions, including hip dysplasia, night blindness, chondrodysplasia (dwarfism that results in deformed limbs), and hypothyroidism. The incidence of these can be reduced by breeders who, in heeding the Malamute Club's Code of Ethics, refrain from breeding affected dogs, and by educated puppy buyers who purchase puppies only from parents that are unaffected by these conditions.

The key word here is "educated." The well-informed buyer will choose puppies whose parents have been certified as free of hip dysplasia by the Orthopedic Foundation for Animals, and of chondrodysplasia by the national breed club. The breeder should further guarantee in the purchase contract that his or her stock is free of the breed's genetic anomalies. The ethical breeder will be impressed by a buyer's knowledge of these potential problems. If the breeder is insulted by your inquiries, look elsewhere.

Health and Temperament

While you may be tempted to purchase or adopt a dog from the first breeder, shelter, or rescue foster home you visit, meeting as many dogs as possible will help you make a more informed choice.

On the health front, look for a dog with clear eyes and a lustrous, uniformly healthy coat, both of which can be effective indicators of internal health and the quality of the dog's diet and breeding. Despite the accepted myth, the dog's nose need not be cool and moist, but the animal should breathe clearly, and her ears should be clean and odor free. Armed with the breed standard, look for a Malamute that closely resembles that ideal, but don't turn the dog down if she doesn't meet or exceed that ideal—no dog does.

Temperament can be trickier, but go with your instincts. When evaluating a litter of puppies, suppress the inclination to "rescue" the shy, timid runt in the corner. A better prospect is the puppy that is friendly and affectionate, outgoing and playful.

Temperament testing can be helpful to a point. Roll the animal over on her back. If she enjoys the position and remains still, she is of a more submissive nature—or may simply be tired at the moment. If she struggles desperately to right herself, she is of a more dominant head and will probably need a stronger, firmer hand to help her understand who is boss. Either one can make a fine pet, but evaluate your own abilities to work with such dogs and make your choice accordingly.

Similar considerations of health and temperament should guide your choice of an older dog, although you may not have the opportunity to visit with the dog's parents, and rolling an unknown 100-pound (45.4 kg) rescue dog over on her back can be extremely dangerous. A rescue or shelter dog, or even a retired show dog, may have a few negative habits to overcome, issues that, ideally, you can discuss with the dog's caretaker to determine whether you are up to the job of rehabilitating such an animal. Indeed, most older dogs have a wart or two, but some are more challenging than others; for example, a three-year-old that is still not housebroken may require a more experienced owner than will a five-year-old that pulls on the leash. More difficult still is the dog that has been mistreated in her past, leaving her with emotional scars that will require time and patience as well as know-how to overcome.

BRINGING YOUR MALAMUTE HOME

Once you have made the fateful decision to bring a Malamute into your home, do all you can to prepare for your new companion's arrival and the life-changing event that it will be. Before you know it, you won't even be able to remember what life was like without a Malamute in the house.

The Puppy Layette

The waiting is almost over. Perhaps you have waited patiently for your new puppy to reach the age at which he can leave his mother, or, after several meetings, you have chosen a rescue Malamute that seems perfectly suited to your family. To ease the anticipation, take a trip to the pet supply store and stock up on what you'll need before your new pet crosses the threshold.

When deciding what supplies you will need to welcome your Malamute, determine first what type of food you will be feeding your new pet. To prevent digestive upset, it is best for the first few days to feed the dog whatever he was being fed before. Then, if you wish to switch to a different food later, do so gradually by mixing the old with the new over several days.

Be warned: Life will never be the same when you bring a new Malamute puppy into the family.

Rounding out the supplies are the standard items:
- ✔ food and water dishes
- ✔ safe and sturdy chew toys (fleece toys, rope bones, sturdy rubber stuffable toys, and Nylabones tend to be favorites)
- ✔ a brush and rake for the coat
- ✔ a leash and collar
- ✔ dog treats
- ✔ puppy shampoo

Don't forget your dog's bed, which will require such items as a crate, blankets, towels, pillows, an exercise pen—whatever you have deemed necessary for your new pet's home within your home. Such preparation will make the adjustment smoother and easier for everyone.

Another very positive gesture is to order identification tags for your dog immediately. You may order these through most pet supply stores and veterinary offices, so start the process now and get the tag on the dog as soon as you can.

Many if not most breeders have their puppies "microchipped" before sending them off to their new homes. This involves the simple insertion of an almost microscopic chip between the animal's shoulder blades, which then provides a high-tech mode for ironclad identification should the dog ever be lost. (If your dog has not been microchipped before coming to live with you, you are wise to look into the procedure yourself; your veterinarian should have the necessary information.) This particular identification method does not, however, replace the need for outfitting your pup with a plain old collar and tags. The ID tag is what most people look for first when they find a lost dog, and it can thus be your pet's ticket home should he ever find himself lost and alone.

Should your new pet become lost, an identification tag will be his ticket home.

The Security of Confinement

Bring your new pet home at the start of a quiet weekend and allow just family and dog to get acquainted. Try and view the situation through the eyes of the dog—a puppy away from his mom and his littermates for the first time, or a rescue dog mourning the separation from his foster family. Obviously, the dog will experience some sort of anxiety, which may translate into certain behaviors the owner deems unacceptable.

While you do not want to reward such behaviors as whimpering, barking, howling, and furniture chewing, you must be sensitive to what the dog is experiencing. Be gentle yet firm—placing a ticking clock outside of your puppy's bed to mimic his mom's heartbeat, for example, or placing your pup's bed near your bed so he can hear you breathing through the night.

The Crate

The most important tool for easing your dog's adjustment into his new home is the concept of confinement, an idea you should begin to introduce from the very first night. Many do this with the help of a crate. Though crates are made for safe airline and car travel, they can work wonders in the day-to-day management of the family pet as well.

While you may cringe at the thought of locking a puppy up in a "box," most dogs actually find their crates—well furnished with warm blankets, padding, and toys—very comforting, assuming the owner does not abuse the crate's use by insisting the dog spend the majority of his time inside it. The crate offers a denlike home to the dog, who may be convinced to try it out with a few treat motivators. Once inside, the dog discovers this isn't so bad after all. You may marvel at how peacefully a new eight-week-old puppy slumbers on that first night away from its family, ensconced in a cozy den carpeted with soft warm blankets.

Successful crate training is rooted in your choice of a properly sized crate. The crate should be large enough to allow the dog to walk in and turn around. Of course there will be a vast difference between the size needed for a young Malamute puppy and the full-sized dog he will become, but you need not purchase more than one. Many crates today come fully equipped with divider panels that allow you to purchase the full-sized crate that you will need for your adult Malamute, while keeping the living space cozy yet expandable for the puppy as he grows.

Other Confinement Areas

Try confining the dog into a specific part of the house at night and whenever you are not at home—perhaps with a roomy exercise pen set up in the kitchen or a corner of your bedroom. This will not only protect the house from a Malamute with an urge to chew furniture legs or tear up carpet on a lonely afternoon, but will also offer the dog his own little corner of the world where he can relax and revel in safety. You may be inspired to adhere to this concept by the fact that a Malamute, particularly a bored Malamute in need of exercise, could decide on a whim to use his almost supercanine strength to tear through the drywall just for fun (which he could do in a confined space, as well; hence the need for the exercise pen, which provides a barrier between dog and household walls). Punishment for such an act would be unjust, especially if you don't catch the dog in the act. This is something the right owner is prepared for and takes steps to try and prevent.

Safety

Confinement can also save a puppy's life, keeping the youngster out of trouble when there is no one to watch out for his safety. When the youngster is allowed to roam, you should ensure that the house has been properly puppyproofed. Make sure electrical cords are hidden, and keep dangerous items, such as poisonous plants and glass Christmas tree ornaments out of the puppy's path. For much of his first year, the young dog will be teething and

To avoid gastric upset, feed your puppy the same food he was fed at his previous home before gradually switching his diet to your dog food of choice.

need desperately to chew. Your job is to ensure that everything he finds to chew on is not only acceptable, but safe, too.

In designing your dog's safe haven, use crates, baby gates, exercise pens or similar modular enclosures, all available at large pet supply stores or through mail order, that will keep the dog confined while still allowing him to walk around and stretch. While most Malamutes relish the opportunity to be indoors if that is where the family is, arrange similar accommodations outdoors as well (you cannot allow the dog to run loose in the neighborhood). Just make sure the fencing material in a fenced yard or kennel run is of the highest quality (Malamutes have been known to chew through chain link), is at least six feet (1.83 m) high, and is

No Chaining, Please

Malamute ownership can be challenging for the owner who cannot provide his or her dog with a secure yard in which to run and play in the great outdoors. Unfortunately, too many dog owners thus decide that chaining the dog in the yard is the next best thing. Well, it isn't.

It's a different story if you intend to be outside with the chained dog, or you leave your pet out for only a brief period of time while you are at home. However, long-term chaining is not only neglectful but danger-ous. It can lead to boredom and aggression in a dog, and it can also place the dog in danger of passersby who decide it might be fun to harass, tease, or even free the poor animal. Safer, more humane alternatives include doggy day care, more frequent walks, more outdoor activities in which you can participate together—whatever you have to do to keep your dog safe, stimulated, and properly exercised.

buried deep enough into the ground to with-stand digging. If your pet is an exceptional jumper, outfit the run with a top, too.

Housebreaking Made Easy

Many a new dog owner shudders at the thought of teaching a new pet where he can eliminate and where he can't, envisioning an endless battle of wills that can severely under-mine the relationship between dog and owner. Indeed, when puppy owners discuss the chal-lenges presented by their new charges, the sub-ject of housebreaking invariably dominates the interchange. Yet there is absolutely no need for such lamentations. Dogs truly want to learn the household rules of elimination, but they can only do so with an owner who is consistent and knowledgeable in how to impart the informa-tion in a way that dogs can understand.

The following are the basic tenets of success-ful housebreaking. Follow them with consistency and patience, and you will soon be proud to proclaim that your dog has been housebroken.

Implement a routine: Where housebreaking is concerned, the routine is the key to success. Puppies must eat several times a day, and thus usually must eliminate on schedule, as well. Feed your pet at the same times every day. Then, after mealtime, take the youngster out-side to a particular corner of the yard where you want him to do his business (you may also choose a newspaper-covered corner of the house, but this will prove to be impractical as the pup grows, so why confuse him now?).

Now give the pup the command *"Go Potty,"* or whatever command you will be comfortable using in the years to come. Yes, dogs can be taught to go on command, and it's never too early to begin the lessons. As soon as the puppy eliminates, praise him profusely so there is no doubt in his mind that he has done something wonderful.

Accentuate the positive: Your mission in this grand endeavor is to make housebreaking a positive experience for yourself and for your dog. Punishment has no place here. Positive reinforcement is all. Praise the dog when he performs properly, and ignore any impulses to punish the animal when he doesn't. When an accident does occur, keep in mind that the mis-take was probably yours. Perhaps the dog didn't understand your expectations, perhaps you missed his signals, perhaps his small bladder had been taxed to its limit, or perhaps the dog could not reach the spot where he knows you wish him to eliminate.

The dog will succeed if given the chance. After meals and whenever you return home from an absence, take the pup immediately to his proper elimination location, give the command, and praise the dog for complying. Watch the dog carefully when he is free to roam the house so you can detect the tell-tale sniffing and crouching that signal nature's call. Be patient and remain consistent in this pattern, and you will find that your puppy, or even your previously untrained adult dog, has been transformed into a gloriously housebroken dog.

Confine the pup: Just as confinement is critical to the safety of a dog, so does it come in equally handy in the challenge that can be housebreaking. In your efforts to make this a positive experience for your dog, keep him confined to a specific area when you are not home to watch his every move. You therefore create more opportunities for praise and less for mistakes.

Dealing with the inevitable: Accidents will happen, of course, but you can turn these accidents into lesson opportunities. Ignore the advice to rub the dog's nose in a calling card he has accidentally left in the house. This will only confuse the poor animal and impede your progress, especially if you punish the dog after he has had his accident (the dog may seem contrite in his behavior, but that is a reaction to *your* behavior, not to what he did hours or even minutes before).

If you do happen to catch the dog in the act of eliminating in the house, react immediately. Make a loud noise to startle the animal and usher him immediately to the proper location where he may finish the job. Again, praise him

Though they may play hard throughout the day, puppies must be allowed breaks for sleep and rest.

enthusiastically, and you will have effectively gotten your point across.

When your dog does have an accident, clean it up quickly. While feces are easily removed, urine can soak into carpeting and similar surfaces and leave a powerful odor that owners find offensive and that invites dogs back again in the future. Use plain soap and water to clean the site of a urine accident or one of the enzymatic cleaners specifically formulated to remove, not mask, the substance. Avoid strong chemical cleaners, especially those that contain ammonia, as these will only intensify the odor.

Establishing the Routine

Just as the routine is key to housebreaking, so is it vital to helping the dog become accustomed to his new home. Even at a very young age, dogs are creatures of habit. They learn quickly to tell time, amazing their owners with their ability to figure out that mealtime is a half hour late, or their tendency to hold a vigil at the front door when it's time for the evening run.

A puppy should be introduced to a wide variety of sights, sounds, and experiences to help him learn what will be expected of him within his new family—and beyond.

that extra time. Is it laundry day? Well, enlist the Malamute to follow you as you carry the clothes to the laundry and encourage the dog to pick up dropped socks and other items (unless he happens to be a dog who enjoys snacking on socks). Such a mix of routine and surprise can result in a Malamute that is well adjusted, content, and secure in the knowledge that his needs will be addressed diligently.

An Indoor/Outdoor Dog

The Alaskan Malamute was bred and raised as a working dog—an Arctic working dog at that. But this does not automatically mean he must be relegated exclusively to the outdoors, never to cross the threshold of the family home. Exile of this type, especially without companionship from another dog (preferably a large dog of the opposite gender) will result in a howling, destructive, and all-around miserable dog.

Yes, this is a big, thick-coated dog. But these are characteristics owners must ponder before choosing to live with this dog who relies on human companionship in all environments, indoors and out. While a young puppy should spend his formative months as an essentially indoor dog, as he grows, he will want to spend more and more time outdoors. As an adult, he will thrive best with balance. The fortunate Malamute is the dog that is offered indoor/outdoor accommodations: regular, though controlled, access to the house and all the wonderful activities that occur there, and to a roomy enclosure in the yard, as well.

The most effective way to ease a new dog into the household is to begin immediately to introduce him to the family patterns so he will learn his place, his role. This offers the dog a sense of security as he learns what to expect of you and what you expect of him, and it imparts the subtle message that you are the boss. One of the greatest mistakes new owners make is overindulging the dog upon his arrival, thus convincing this extremely pack-sensitive breed that he is welcome to take on the leadership role.

To establish the routine, determine how and when you will be caring for the dog, and carry out those various duties at the same times every day. Remain true, too, to scheduled daily exercise, and do the same with daily training sessions.

Maintain the element of freshness by involving the dog in other, typically non-routine activities, as well. Do you have any household repair jobs to tend to? Let your Malamute join in. Sure, the dog's assistance may cause the job to last twice as long, but the joy the animal exhibits as he takes part in the action is worth

New Experiences

A new Malamute in the family has the grand responsibility of getting to know the intimate world within his family pack, as well as the world beyond his front door. Just imagine all he must learn. Assist the dog in this mission, and you will help foster the development of a wonderfully well-adjusted pet who is prepared to accompany you wherever you go.

New Places, New Faces

One word you are likely to hear whenever puppies are discussed is "socialization." Although the Alaskan Malamute is a naturally affectionate dog, he is prone to dominant, even aggressive behavior in adulthood if overindulged as a puppy. Intensive socialization efforts should be started as early as possible.

This can be an immensely enjoyable process, in which you expose the puppy to new experiences, places, and people—all with a very positive flair. Reward the youngster for his positive response to such new explorations, yet remain firm and consistent in handling the puppy both at home and away. Take the puppy with you wherever you go (if possible), and allow everyone to pet and play with him so he might learn just how satisfying life can be. Of course the pup must also learn to be alone to prevent him from suffering in the future from separation anxiety, which can manifest in barking, chewing, and all-around destruction.

Because Malamutes don't always get along with others of their own kind (especially males with males and females with females), introduce the pup to other dogs. Larger dogs are usually preferable to smaller dogs in this endeavor, as smaller dogs may be seen as prey to the predatory Malamute. Allow the pup to play and wrestle and learn just how delightful others of his own kind can be. Invite friends and family to your house frequently, so the puppy will also grow accustomed to human visitors.

Other Animals

Through diligent attention to socialization, you might be able to squelch the Malamute's innate predatory tendencies somewhat by introducing a young puppy to other animals, which is especially critical if this dog will be living with cats. Savvy breeders and Malamute rescuers recommend that all Malamute puppies be socialized with cats. Malamutes raised with cats tend to be less predatory toward the feline species, which can be a benefit somewhere down the line if the dog needs to go to a new home where cats reside.

Loud Noises

Finally, enhance your socialization program by exposing the dog to everyday household noises. If your pup happens to be afraid of loud noises, introduce him gradually and positively to such sounds as a vacuum cleaner or a blender. Expose the dog to these imagined threats gradually for increasing periods of time,

WORDS OF WISDOM

Never leave a Malamute alone with others of his own kind. While the rule about never leaving children alone with dogs is standard for *all* dogs, Malmutes, despite their history as team-oriented sled dogs (or, perhaps, because of it), are prone to fighting with one another over food and possessions, with ugly results.

reward him with treats along the way, and you should be able to convince the animal that he has nothing to fear.

Visiting the Veterinarian

Another component to socialization is introducing the puppy to the veterinarian, thus launching a relationship that will remain a constant throughout the dog's life. There will be ample opportunity to forge this relationship during the first few months when the puppy must visit the veterinarian every few weeks for his vaccinations and physical examinations.

By about six months of age, the puppy should visit the veterinarian for spaying or neutering. Done early, altering can substantially reduce the incidence of various cancers later in a dog's life. But whether visiting the veterinarian for minor altering surgery, or for a quick injection, make each experience pleasurable and positive for the dog. Bring treats, and behave in an upbeat, enthusiastic manner that will help the dog build positive associations with the veterinary office. Even though the dog may understand that this is where "shots" occur, convince him through positive reinforcement that this place isn't so bad after all. A dog so convinced will be far more willing to return in the future.

Everyday Habits

Dogs are not whelped automatically understanding the adjustments they will have to make that are inherent to being a pet dog in our society. During his first few weeks of life, for example, the young puppy has no idea that soon he will be asked to walk cooperatively with his owner, led by a leash of leather or nylon. It is the owner's job to teach the pup this skill, as always with patience and positive reinforcement.

Walking on leash: Begin these lessons as early as possible, first by introducing the puppy to the collar, which he should wear at all times. Occasionally snap the leash to the collar and allow the pup to walk around the house dragging the leash behind him. Once he has grown accustomed to this, hold the leash to allow the pup to get used to that new sensation. Keep all sessions short. Rewarded with praise and treats as he masters the art of walking on leash, the dog's greatest reward will be the increased freedom he enjoys as his behavior earns him access to a wide range of locales.

Grooming: Similar early attention should be given to grooming. The earlier a puppy is introduced to brushing, bathing, ear cleaning, tooth brushing, and nail clipping, the more cooperative he will be toward these when he weighs in at 90 or 100 pounds (41–45.4 kg) and is far more capable of fighting the hand that grooms him. When grooming is introduced early and positively, the dog will also learn how pleasurable grooming time can be. As an added bonus, your dog's cooperation with your efforts reinforces the fact that you are in charge and that he must in turn lie still as you or the groomer brush him or clip his nails.

Toys and Games

Dogs cannot live by food and water alone. They need toys, too, and a wide variety from which to choose. Beginning with their penchant for chew toys as puppies, a necessity to help them through the teething process, most will blossom into adulthood with a healthy affection for playthings and games.

You will be wise to teach the puppy early on that some items belong to the dog and some belong to the human family members, the

Your Malamute must have an ample supply of chew toys available.

latter being off limits to the pooch. Make sure the dog always has access to his own collection of toys that are safe, sturdy, and free of small parts that might become casualties of vigorous play and lodge in a canine throat or intestine.

As renowned as he is for his dignity, the Malamute is equally famous for his sense of humor—he loves games. Keep this in mind during your own games of football, baseball, Frisbee, and the like, in which you can invite your Malamute to participate. Keep control of the situation, however, and avoid such aggressive games as tug-of-war, which can overstimulate the dog and become a test of dominance between dog and owner.

Rely on your creativity to design Malamute games. Consider hide-and-seek, for example. Upon recruiting a Malamute as your playmate, he will quickly understand that he is to wait (*stay*) while you hide. Then call the dog to you. With great gusto he will seek you out, his reward being that moment when he finds the person he loves most in the world hiding in a closet or behind a door.

TIP

Caution

You are wise not to use socks as dog toys. Not only does this teach a dog to chew on clothing, it also satisfies the insatiable taste some dogs have for socks, which, when swallowed can cause potentially fatal intestinal blockages.

The Boarding Kennel

There comes a time in every dog owner's life when he or she must leave home for a destination that, heaven forbid, does not allow dogs. Fortunately, in this day and age there are several options available for what to do with the dog when you are away.

While you may call in a pet sitter to feed and walk the dog at your own home several times a day, another very popular option is the boarding kennel. This may be a kennel operated by a veterinary hospital or a breeder, or one of the luxury pet hotels that cater to the canine species. Whichever type of kennel you choose, check out the premises ahead of time for cleanliness and space, ask about the diet and exercise that is provided, and remember that reservations are usually mandatory during holidays and other peak travel times.

BECOMING YOUR MALAMUTE'S BEST FRIEND

There is no sure-fire recipe for forging an indelible bond between an Alaskan Malamute and her family, but getting to know who she is and where she comes from is an important step toward setting the foundation for a long and satisfying relationship.

The Importance of the Pack

There are few breeds as sensitive to the protocols of pack order as the Alaskan Malamute. From the moment this dog enters a new household, whether she is an eight-week-old puppy or a five-year-old adult, she will be unable to rest until she knows where she belongs in the family hierarchy. If you ignore the dog's need to find her place, you shirk your duties in letting your pet know that you are the leader, or alpha, and the Malamute will gladly accept that role for herself. This dog, even at a very young age, will recognize immediately if you vacillate or are in any way unsure in your resolve, and she will take advantage of the opportunity.

A well-trained Malamute can enjoy a variety of activities and, because of that, enjoy a more peaceful, fulfilling home life.

But just how do you assert your role as leader to this potentially domineering and very large dog? Some believe that physical punishment and cruelty are the answer. They're not. Treatment of that sort will only foster a timid or overly aggressive Malamute that in every way violates what this dog and her bond to the human species are meant to be.

The answer is far less traumatic. Remain firm, patient, and consistent in your interactions with the dog. When you give your dog a command, insist that she obey it. At bedtime, make sure she understands, every single night without exception, that you have your bed and the dog has her bed. If the dog decides she wants to jump up on you (a potential hazard when she hits the 90 lb. [41 kg] mark), let her know, with a loud *"Off"* or *"Down"* and a step backward, that this will never be allowed.

In time, this extremely intelligent, sensitive animal will realize that you are the leader. Period. The dog may continue to challenge and test you just to make sure you really mean it, but when she does, your response must be the same—consistently. You must not waver. You will then be rewarded with a dog that is content and confident in knowing her place.

While the mechanics of establishing the family pack sound simple enough, many owners, especially when faced with an adorable puppy that simply wants to wiggle and play and lick the faces of her family, decide that the training can wait. But the puppy's mother doesn't see it that way. She begins to mold the character of her pups immediately, and now you must take over that responsibility for her, whether you are dealing with a young puppy or a mature adult Malamute.

The Stages of Development

As a dog matures, she travels through different stages of development, most of which closely resemble the stages of human development. Recognizing and understanding those stages will help you better deal with and appreciate this great animal through all her wondrous transitions.

Puppyhood

The puppy comes into the world blind, relatively immobile, completely helpless. A fledgling predator, she relies on her mother's care during her first few weeks of life. She is her source of food, warmth, and survival. Then, at about four or five weeks of age, her eyes open, she takes notice of the world, and makes primitive attempts to interact both with her littermates and other treasures in her environment. She may initiate games of tug-of-war with a sister or chew happily on a brother's ear, all the while venturing further and further from the safety and security of Mom. Yet she is never far, ready to intervene in order to instruct her young on the rules of acceptable behavior.

At about eight weeks of age, the puppy is weaned and, assuming Mom was nurturing and attentive, ready emotionally to make the leap to a new human family. Once installed in her new home, the puppy should continue to be instructed in manners and deportment, now by her human mom. Through her first few months she will joyfully follow you from room to room, eagerly learning who is who in the family pack, mastering the ropes of housebreaking, and even beginning to learn the basic commands.

Adolescence

Somewhere between four and six months of age, the puppy will enter adolescence. Physically she will lose that soft puppy coat, and her ears will suddenly seem too large for her head, her legs too long for her body. But even more striking is the fact that the once sweet, willing, and attentive puppy will suddenly begin to ignore her owner's requests and will seem to have forgotten all she has learned to this point. Anyone who has witnessed or experienced human adolescence is well aware of the symptoms.

Adolescence can be a challenging time for the owner of the growing Malamute. As the dog attempts to assert herself, the owner may wonder why he or she ever thought getting a dog was a good idea. Indeed, frustration can lend an unpleasant aura to the relationship, but stick with it and remain consistent and firm. The

On a warm summer day, the Malamute may prefer to rest on a bed of ice rather than take a dip in the backyard pool.

young dog will ultimately acquiesce, understanding that you obviously mean business.

Try and look at the bright side. This is a time of great physical development, during which you suddenly see that yes, this is going to be a large, athletic dog. While she may be guided by a stubborn streak at the moment, she is also thrilled to be invited to participate in new games and activities—longer walks, preliminary sledding exercises, and so on—that were not appropriate for a young puppy. By sharing these experiences, you may channel those abundant adolescent energies into positive directions, and continue to forge the strong foundation upon which your relationship will rest in the future. In the meantime, keep your sense of humor. This, too, shall pass.

Maturity

As a large breed, the Alaskan Malamute may take longer to mature than will her smaller counterparts. She may not fill out fully until about two years of age, and her mental development may take even longer. The young adult Malamute should be exuberant and active. Even if you have remained consistent in her training, her *joie de vivre* may still get the best of her at times; however, she should be more settled, and yes, cooperative, than she was as an adolescent.

By age five or six, the Malamute that has enjoyed proper training and care should be well settled into maturity. The dog has finally made it through her formative stages, she knows who she is, and she wants nothing more than to live as companion and partner to her human family members. Some of the breed's enthusiasts think this is the ideal age to bring a new Malamute into the family, considering the mature Alaskan Malamute to be one of the finest pets dogdom has to offer.

A Positive Approach

Just as owners must pledge to remain consistent in their treatment of their Alaskan Malamute, so must they simultaneously commit to a positive philosophy of training. Harsh physical or otherwise negative training methods require more effort and reap poor results.

The Malamute is a sensitive soul that, though stubborn at times, will understand very quickly what is being asked of her. Making training a positive, fun, and interesting activity can help to accomplish this.

Trained via positive reinforcement, the dog learns that there are pleasant rewards for behaving in certain ways. She is motivated to perform or to behave, not by fear, pain, or threats, but by the rewards she enjoys from doing so. This begins when she learns she will be praised profusely for not eliminating on the living room carpet, but out in the backyard. She learns to sit on command because this pleases her owner, evident in the fact that she also receives a favored treat when she obeys the command. She learns to walk on a leash because that means she gets to go out and explore the world.

Such a focus on all that is positive can even help correct annoying habits. Behaviorist William Campbell, who has employed this philosophy quite successfully, recommends that owners use what he calls the "jolly routine." Imagine that you have a dog that barks at the postal carrier each day. When you spot the innocent victim coming up the walk, attract your dog's attention by behaving in a silly, "jolly" way: Tickle the dog, praise the dog, be the clown, offer a treat. In time, the dog will associate the postal carrier's arrival with your joyful behavior and treats, and no longer feel the need to bark.

Training with a positive focus is not only a more humane way to go, but is far more pleasant—and safe—for the owner. How rewarding to know that one need not physically punish or react angrily to a dog for her to progress. In fact, if you choose the negative path, you are likely to make no progress at all with the Malamute, or any dog.

Puppy Kindergarten

Not too long ago, the standard practice was to wait until a puppy reached six months of age before beginning her formal training. But as we've seen, her mom begins right away, and so should we.

This philosophy has been institutionalized in the past couple of decades in the emergence of a special type of puppy training class referred to as "puppy kindergarten" or "puppy preschool." Welcoming puppies as young as three months of age (who have had most of their vaccinations), these classes promote socialization and intro-duce the young students to basic commands.

Each class typically begins with a play ses-sion, during which the puppies have the oppor-tunity to wrestle and tumble together. While this helps the puppies expend the excess energy that could interrupt their concentration once the formal part of class begins, so does it intro-duce them to other puppies of all sizes, shapes, and colors, teaching them that other dogs are to be playmates not opponents.

Once the play session is over, class begins. The trick to teaching young puppies is to keep the sessions short, lively, and rich with treat rewards that keep the puppies' attention. Most newcomers to puppy kindergarten class are amazed at how fascinated young puppies can be with the mechanics of such a formally struc-tured class, and how quickly and willingly they can learn to sit, lie down, stay, and come on command. Educated as youngsters, they will be far more successful students later when they enter a more traditional obedience class

Puppy kindergarten/preschool, which addresses the special world view of young puppies, is a great way to introduce your Malamute to a lifetime of learning.

designed for older puppies. They will be better pets at home, too, for training of this type rein-forces your role as leader and the puppy's role as partner, teammate, and companion.

While you may employ the tenets of puppy kindergarten training at home on your own—and you must hold short homework sessions each day between classes to reinforce the lessons—the class environment is superior because of the socialization factor.

Finding the Proper Trainer

It takes a village to raise a Malamute prop-erly. That is how it has always been since the days when the dogs literally lived in Inuit vil-lages in the Arctic, and it remains true today. This gregarious, people-loving dog's contempo-rary village is comprised first of the breeder who takes great care in bringing her into the world, followed by the carefully chosen owners who become the dog's home pack, and finally by the trainers who will instruct her in her basic manners and in the skills necessary for such activities as mushing or weight pulling should you decide you would like to see your dog participate in those traditional pursuits.

While it would indeed be a perfect world if all dogs were enrolled in obedience classes, this is especially critical for the Alaskan Malamute. Although they may not typically meet the criteria required for the obedience show ring, Malamutes do require training to give them a sense of structure and security. Attend obedience classes throughout the Malamute's first two years of life—or for the first year or two after an adult Malamute joins your family. Working together this way not only teaches the dog basic commands, but also strengthens the bond between the dog and her owner.

What to Look For

When seeking a trainer for your Malamute, look for someone who has experience working with this breed—or at least with some type of large, strong-willed dog, ideally of the Nordic variety. Avoid the trainer who bashes the breed for a lack of brains, who prescribes to obsolete, not to mention counterproductive, force-training methods, or who cringes during an initial meeting when you mention your dog's breed. A superior candidate is that individual who smiles at the name of the breed and relishes the challenge of working with such a dog. Another good sign is the trainer who would prefer that the whole family attend the class to ensure that all are properly prepared to guide and interact effectively with this unique animal.

In addition to evaluating a prospective trainer's Malamute IQ, ask about his or her training philosophy and methods. You have a vested interest in how your dog will be treated, and if you suspect the methods employed will be too harsh for your or your dog's liking, or if you sense the trainer is looking for shortcuts, perhaps with gimmicky gadgets, such as prong collars on young puppies, rather than pursuing solid, permanent teaching and behavior modification, look elsewhere.

And finally, determine if you are compatible with the trainer, too. Dog training classes are essentially designed more for the training of the owner than of the dog, for once the class is over, it's up to the owner to continue and reinforce the lessons. If you are uncomfortable with the trainer, you probably won't learn as effectively as you might with someone who sets you at ease.

Training Tenets

Positive reinforcement: Malamutes are quick to master any number of skills, yet most training finds its roots in the fundamentals of obedience. A variety of methods exist on how best to train, but in keeping with the tenets of positive reinforcement, it's usually more effective to encourage the dog to do what you want her to do rather than punishing her for what you don't want her to do. You will probably find it easiest to reward the dog with treats, to keep

WORDS OF WISDOM

Not every dog views food as the ultimate reward in training. You may find that your dog is more motivated by a special toy that you present only during training sessions.

the training sessions short and interesting, and to set aside time every day for training. And ignore the myth that you can't teach an old dog new tricks. You can teach any dog new tricks, as most find working with their owners in this way quite rewarding. You may just have to be more patient with the older dog that is more likely to be set in her ways.

Special training collars: You may also find it effective to use a special collar for training, perhaps a chain training collar (preferable to the prong collar, which is unnecessary for most dogs, and painful when employed by unskilled novices). The chain collar should not be used on puppies younger than six months of age whose neck muscles might not yet be fully developed, and it should be used for training or walking only; if you use it as the dog's everyday collar, the dog might choke or hang herself. When the dog sees you approach with the collar, she will know that it's time for training.

The chain training collar must be placed on the dog correctly for optimum comfort and results. Fit the chain through an end ring, forming a loop. When facing the dog, hold the collar's loop open; it should be the shape of a backward "6." Place it over the dog's head. Correctly positioned on a dog that is walking on your left side, the chain will tighten when you pull on the leash, and loosen automatically when you release that pressure.

But the chain collar is not the only collar available for training. Depending on the dog's temperament, you might consider one of many different styles that have been developed for teaching a dog to behave. These include the slip collar, a milder version of a "choke collar," which exerts only mild pressure and is more easily released; the head halter, designed to prevent a

Consistent training, coupled with positive reinforcement and socialization, can result in a dog who is a joy to have around the house.

dog from pulling on the leash by focusing control on the animal's head and muzzle; or various harness designs that can reduce pulling by changing the dog's center of gravity as she walks. Consult with your dog's trainer on what might be best for your pet, and keep in mind that he or she may simply prefer a traditional buckle collar coupled with lots of verbal communication and positive reinforcement.

An enclosed area: Choose an enclosed area for training that is far from such distractions as baseball games or a traffic-filled street.

Some training methods require that you pull or push the dog into the proper positions with a training collar and your hands. But if you refrain from touching the dog, the training

A barking or howling Malamute may need more stimulus to avoid boredom.

behaviorist and a committed owner, such dogs can learn to recognize the error of their ways and act to preserve their place in the family—and perhaps save their lives.

The major problems that lead to such a tragic end are incessant barking (or, in the case of the Malamute, incessant howling), digging, chewing, and aggression. In virtually every case where a behavior problem leads to the premature dissolution of the dog/owner relationship, there is a reason for the dog's behavior. When that dog is a large, robust Malamute, the result can be massive destruction—perhaps ruining a wall or a carved wooden banister—for which the owner was totally unprepared. In most such cases, the problem can be remedied, simply by recognizing the underlying cause and directing the dog's attention and energy in more positive directions.

Barking: That barking dog, for instance, is most likely lonely, the unwitting victim of perhaps well-meaning owners who don't realize that they cannot just keep the dog in the yard day in and day out with little or no companionship and even less exercise. Such a dog is in need of more attention from and activity with its family, perhaps the services of a good daycare center, or a large canine companion of the opposite gender.

Chewing: As for the Olympian chewer, it is usually a younger dog that is experiencing the irritation of teething and is lacking a sufficient collection of appropriate chew toys. She thus relieves the irritation on table legs, leather shoes, or anything she finds. A lonely or similarly unhappy adult dog may also resort to chewing, doing a great deal of damage in the process. This dog, too, needs more activity in its

might stick more effectively because the dog is more inclined to believe that her actions are her own idea. Above all, remember that you must never lose your temper. Sometimes it can take days to convince a Malamute to comply with your requests, but remain calm, firm, patient, and consistent. If the dog is distracted or refuses to cooperate, have her obey one more command, end the session, and resume when you are both more amenable to working.

A Positive Look at Behavior Problems

Every year, millions of dogs, including Alaskan Malamutes, are dispatched to the nation's animal shelters because they have developed behavioral problems that their owners are either unwilling or unable to correct. In most cases, with just a little bit of attention from a skilled life, and plenty of safe and sturdy chew toys on which to vent pent-up energies and aggressions.

Digging: Employ a similar tactic in the handling of the dog that digs, which many a Malamute does either out of frustration or the sheer joy of it. Here again the dog may need more exercise and companionship. You may also satisfy the dog's cravings by providing a section of the yard that she can dig up to her heart's content. Bury toys or bones in the Malamute digging pit to teach your dog that this is her special spot, and if the dog begins digging elsewhere, move her to the legal area and encourage her to go at it. Remember, when faced with behavior problems, providing alternatives and channeling the dog's energies in more positive directions is far superior to, and more productive than, punishment.

Aggression: The overly aggressive dog is potentially dangerous, especially if her aggression is directed toward family members. There are many reasons for such tendencies, and most cases are best addressed with the help of an experienced canine behaviorist. He or she is best able to diagnose the cause and prescribe the proper therapy for correcting the problem. But, sadly, sometimes the situation has gone too far, the dog is too severely affected and possibly dangerous, and the safest remedy is euthanasia.

Kids and Malamutes

For centuries Malamutes have held a special affinity for children, and the feelings are mutual. Still, you must exercise the same caution you would with any dog when children are involved. Namely, never leave the dog, even the most trustworthy Malamute, alone and unattended with children, and make the effort to teach your kids how to behave around dogs—both their own and others they meet on the street.

It is not unusual today to be out on a walk with a dog and be accosted by children who run toward you screaming in their delight to see "the doggie." These children have not been taught how to approach strange dogs and will probably soon be added to the ever-growing list of America's dog-bite casualties.

On the flip side is the child who quietly approaches and asks to pet your dog. This child, having been taught appropriate manners, usually knows to allow the dog to sniff his or her hand first. The child then pets the dog on the shoulder or side where the animal can monitor his or her movements, rather than patting her on the top of the head, out of the dog's field of vision. Teaching your children these protocols, as well as how to care for and handle their own puppies and dogs properly, will ensure that they will not be party to a dog-bite event, many of which are more the fault of the children (and thus the parents) than they are of the dog.

The New Baby and the Malamute

Other related mistakes occur when owners bring a new baby into a home with a resident dog who has long occupied an important niche in the family pack. Far too many new parents mistakenly believe that now that a child is around, the dog must be exiled to the backyard. The dog in turn grows resentful of the child, to whom she may not have even been formally introduced. A more productive tactic is to make the dog a part of the baby's life from the very beginning. Introduce her to the small bundle as soon as you bring the baby home. Allow the dog to grow accustomed to the newcomer's scent and to accompany you when it's time for feedings, diaper changes, baths, and walks.

HOW-TO: THE BASIC

What follows are the basic commands that every dog should know and one method you can use to teach them. Once the dog has mastered these, she may expand her repertoire—and her vocabulary—into such commands as *"Shake"* (as in to "shake" paws), *"Roll over,"* and *"Speak,"* and of course the various commands associated with mushing and similarly athletic activities.

Sit

When using the treat-reward system to teach the *sit,* the first and simplest command to teach, you can use a treat to "trick" the puppy into sitting. Approach the standing puppy and show her the treat in your hand. Move the treat back up over the puppy's head while saying *"Sit."* As the puppy follows the treat with her eyes and her nose, she suddenly finds she is sitting. Praise the pup and give a reward.

Down

Place the dog in a *sit* and again, tantalize her with the treat in your hand. Once her attention is on the treat held near her nose, move your hand slowly and vertically down to the floor while issuing the *down* command. The dog will naturally follow the treat down to the point where she is lying on the ground, for which she will receive both praise and the treat as her reward.

Stay/Come

Stay and *come* are most easily taught together. First, with the dog in a *sit,* back away slowly while giving the *stay* command. Move back only a short distance, say the command again, then return slowly to the dog and praise and reward her for having stayed put. Gradually lengthen the distance you move back, and soon the dog will not have any doubt what *"Stay"* means.

Once the dog seems to have mastered the *stay,* you can add the *come.* After you have backed away and praised the dog verbally for staying, issue the *come* command. You may have to embellish this by slapping your thigh and calling the dog to you in a joyful, playful voice. If all else fails, offer a treat, anything to let the dog know that you want her to come to you. When she does, praise and rewards are in order. Once the dog understands the command, you should be able to replace the happy routine with a simple *come* command.

Come is an important command because, even though your dog should not be out and about off leash, there may be times when you need

Hold a treat up above the head of a standing Malamute and move your hand backward. The dog will automatically follow the moving treat with her head and suddenly find herself in a sitting position.

to call her to you, and it's comforting to think that she will indeed obey. When practicing, if the dog refuses, or simply takes her sweet time in getting over to you, resist the temptation to scold or punish the dog when she finally obeys. This will confuse the dog—she came to you, however slowly, when you called her, only to be punished. If you intend to scold the dog for noncompliance, go to the dog instead of calling her to you. Malamutes are too smart to come willingly for a scolding. Remain consistent and clear in your messages.

Heel

As large sled dogs that are bred and born to pull, heeling does not necessarily come naturally to the Malamute. Frankly, some trainers do not even see the need for a dog to walk perfectly at your heels, preferring instead to see a dog that is free to explore without pulling on the leash and dragging an unwitting owner down the sidewalk, causing a downright dangerous situation.

A dog in a perfect *heel* walks to the left of her owner, the leash loose and hanging in the shape of a J. With much work, you might get a Malamute to fit this picture, but for most owners, just getting the dog not to pull will suffice. Again, treats can come in handy for this, holding the treat down at your side to attract the dog's attention, and praising her for walking without pulling.

You can also try this exercise: Walk forward with the dog and then suddenly do an about-face, either to the side or to the rear. This will pull the dog into a new direction and perhaps startle her. Do this several times (with praise and rewards, of course), and soon the dog will understand that she should be watching you to see what you might do. In so doing, she refrains

If you don't intend to show your dog in conformation, she may not need to learn the perfect heel. Simply learning to walk nicely on the leash without pulling is sufficient for most pet Malamutes.

from pulling on the leash and becomes more attentive to the person at the other end.

Fetch

In teaching this ever-popular play command, toss a favorite toy, and command the dog to *fetch* it. Once she complies, call the dog enthusiastically back to you. When she returns to you, the dog may not understand that she should then give the item to you. Convince her to do so, perhaps by offering her a treat as a replacement and by using the command *Drop it.* This can turn into an enjoyable game for all involved, and it may ultimately blossom into a handy household skill, as well. For example, if you are doing laundry and drop a sock en route from the hamper to the washer, just ask the dog to *fetch* it and bring it to you for washing. The dog—a working breed, remember—will be pleased to help, or pleased to take the sock and run. It all depends on her sense of humor at the moment.

FEEDING A VERY LARGE DOG

When one beholds the vision that is the healthy Alaskan Malamute, the signs are unmistakable. The dog walks with confidence in his step, propelled forward by a combination of strong, hard bones and powerful muscles. His eyes are clear and bright, his coat thick and lustrous. This dog is obviously receiving a diet rich in the high-quality nutrients needed to cut that figure of energy and health.

The History of Malamute Feeding

Historically, throughout most of their domestic relationship with humans, dogs typically received our leftovers. They may have helped their humans track and hunt their prey, but generally to the humans went the bulk of the spoils. This pattern was particularly evident among Arctic sled dogs that would share their people's food, yet receive just enough to fuel their rigorous winter duties on the snow and ice, their rations then cut back severely during summer "vacation" to an amount just enough to keep them alive.

The noble wolf-like countenance of the Alaskan Malamute is the result of solid, high-quality nutrition and proper feeding practices.

Although the Arctic people, as well as others throughout the world who lived with dogs, understood that canine performance depended on fuel, few consciously worried about balance or nutrients. Even a few decades ago, with only a handful of brands of commercial dog foods on the market, dog owners rarely gave a thought to what might be in that can or in that bag. Even veterinary schools devoted very little time to the importance of nutrition.

Thankfully, times have changed substantially since the dark ages of canine nutrition. We now know that the content and quality of the foods that go into the dog will eventually make themselves evident externally in the dog's appearance, behavior, and performance. Because we have come to realize that nutrition offers us an easy barometer of canine health, it receives much more respect these days, evident in the

high-quality commercial foods now available not only to satisfy our dogs' appetites, but to help them enjoy optimum health and longevity.

Basic Nutritional Building Blocks

Despite how it might look at first glance, dogs are not true carnivores. They, like us, are omnivores, meaning they fare best on a ration comprised of both meat and vegetable material. If you opt to feed the domestic dog nothing but meat, the detrimental effects of this will become quickly apparent in the dog's coat, eyes, and demeanor.

This may seem a puzzling concept considering that the domestic dog occupies only one branch of a large canid family tree, whose other

The properly fed Malamute shines with health, contentment, and vitality.

branches house such wild, profoundly meat-eating dogs as wolves, foxes, coyotes, and the like. But, as wildlife biologists know, even these wild meat eaters relish some vegetation in their diets, collected from the digestive tracts of their herbivorous prey.

The magical combination of animal and vegetable material offers the dog the full complement of nutrients he requires. These include proteins, fats, carbohydrates, vitamins, minerals, and water, each of which plays a critical role in the operation of the dog's system.

Protein

Whether derived from plant or animal sources, protein is a fundamental building block of the canine diet; but all proteins are not created equal, and herein lies the challenge.

With commercial dog foods, you often get what you pay for. If you seek the least expensive brand, you will probably also wind up with the poorest quality protein, thus sacrificing the health of your dog's bones, muscle, blood, and countless other tissues and organs. While the dog's protein needs will change during the course of his life, the young puppy and the high-powered athlete requiring more protein than the sedentary senior, all need the highest-quality protein, and none can afford the physical degeneration poor-quality food can cause.

Fats

Despite its bad press, fat is an essential nutrient in the canine diet, required to fuel the dog's energy needs, which, for a working Malamute, can be substantial. As with protein, fat needs will differ from dog to dog, depending on age and career (e.g., sled dog, weight puller, etc.). But whether the dietary fat comes from either plant or animal sources, overnourishing a dog, any dog, with fat (most commonly accomplished by plying the dog with table scraps from the human dinner table) will lead to a fat dog and yet another contribution to the serious obesity problem in America's canine population.

Carbohydrates

A dog's energy needs are not fueled by fats alone. Assisting them in this job are carbohydrates, although carbs are not typically as high in energy as are fats. Carbohydrates are prominent players in most commercial dog food formulations, present in such key ingredients as corn, rice, and barley. They play an important role in both the working Malamute's ability to travel long distances over the ice and snow, and the companion Malamute's afternoon spent competing in agility.

Vitamins and Minerals

A great many dog owners succumb to the advertising promises that particular vitamin and/or mineral supplements are what dogs need for complete and balanced nutrition. This, however, is not true if the dog is receiving one of the high-quality, "complete and balanced" commercial dog foods currently on the market. What all dog owners are wise to realize is that oversupplementing dogs can be just as damaging as undernourishing them. We must fight that natural human inclination that holds if a little is good, more must surely be better.

That "more" can be dangerous if the vitamins being supplemented are the fat-soluble A or D. Unlike the water-soluble Bs and C (the latter of

which some breeders supplement to enhance calcium metabolism in Malamutes), which are flushed through the body each day, vitamins A and D accumulate in the tissues and end up preventing the beneficial functions they are meant to facilitate.

Minerals as supplements can also bring negative results. Consider, for instance, calcium, a mineral instrumental in bone growth. If you decide that your dog should have more calcium in his diet, you will throw phosphorus off kilter, as the two must be balanced to perform their duties properly. You are better off leaving the chemistry to the experts and reaping the benefits of their research by feeding your dog a high-quality commercial diet that fits the "complete and balanced" criteria.

Fish as a supplement: There is, however, one type of "supplement" that some Malamute breeders have come to recommend. Looking to the history of their breed, and hence to its historically fish-heavy diet, which was radically changed to grain-based nutrition as soon as the dog was brought down into the lower 48 states, some have suspected that perhaps a weekly supplemental ration of fish (say, one-quarter of a can of mackerel) would provide their dogs with a more Malamute-friendly form of iodine. This is not simply breeder folklore either, as selected manufacturers of commercial pet foods have begun to add fish oil, and fish itself, to some of their foods to enhance coat and skin health, an addition devotees of Nordic breeds see as a positive step for their dogs.

Water

One may not expect to find water included in a list of dietary building blocks for dogs, but without the presence of simple H_2O each and every day, none of the other nutrients can be metabolized or transported throughout the body. In fact, water is itself the prime component of the dog's body ensuring that the biological system reaches the level of optimum performance.

Unfortunately, Malamutes don't always care to drink when they should, especially when the mercury dips below the freezing point on a frosty morning, and the Malamute team is anxious to take off pulling a sled through the snow. However, these dogs, as well as any dog about to embark on a demanding activity, must lap up an ample supply of water before they begin and throughout the day.

WORDS OF WISDOM

When your Malamute isn't all that interested in drinking his water, take a hint from mushers who know: Spike the water with some sort of irresistible flavoring agent (unsalted meat broth or stock is always a favorite). No self-respecting dog can turn down such a treat, and no self-respecting owner should allow any dog ever to face an empty water dish.

What to Feed

So you have committed yourself to providing your Malamute with a healthy, well-balanced diet, only to find that there are now hundreds of brands of foods on the market. You cannot simply close your eyes and choose, because just as proteins are not all created equal, neither are all the dog foods that contain those many proteins.

An Easy Transition

The first step toward choosing the brand of dog food is to consult your dog's breeder or previous caretaker. For the first few days or weeks in your home, the puppy or dog should receive the food he was fed before coming into your household, even if that is not what you would like to see your pet eat in the future.

Once you believe the time is right to switch the dog over to the new food, do so gradually over the course of several days. Each day, mix more and more of the new food in with the old until finally the entire dish is filled with the new food. This way your dog need not suffer the gastric upset a sudden change can cause, especially during what can be a very emotionally trying time for the dog.

Labeling

The next tool you may use in choosing your dog's food is the label on the package, but even this can be confusing if you don't know what to look for. On the positive side of this quandary, you can usually assume that if you go with a well-known brand, you will not be harming your dog. These foods are formulated by teams of veterinary nutritionists and scientists, who have invested a great deal of time, money, and effort into determining what dogs need nutritionally and formulating foods to meet those needs. By

A constant supply of fresh, clean water is the cornerstone of the proper canine diet and responsible canine care.

learning to decipher the labels, you can decide whether a food you are considering falls into this category.

By law, a dog food's label must include several key components:

✔ It must indicate the name of the species for which the food is intended.

✔ It must include a guaranteed analysis of the crude protein, crude fat, crude fiber, and moisture content of the food.

✔ It must offer an ingredients list that spells out ingredients in descending order of content.

✔ It must carry a nutritional "mission" statement, such as "complete and balanced for all life stages," or "complete and balanced for growth."

But we must look between the lines to determine the quality of the ingredients—especially of the proteins—and this is where a little knowledge can help. Specifically, look for a statement about Association of American Feed Control Officials protocols on the package, and you're on the right track.

While the simple words "beef" or "chicken by-products" on a label won't tell you much about the quality of those ingredients, a statement about AAFCO standards can. The AAFCO sets minimum and maximum nutritional guidelines for pet foods for various life stages, so look for a food that states it meets those standards, and does so through the test feeding of dogs. Such information does not guarantee that this will be the perfect food for your dog, or even that it is a food of the highest possible quality, but, as a guideline, it's a step in the right direction.

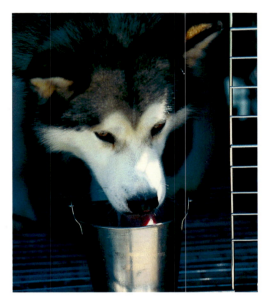

Food Types

Once you have chosen the brand of food you would like to try, you must then decide whether to feed your dog dry food, semimoist patties, canned food, or a combination.

Dry kibble is by far the most popular type of dog food, and it can handily nourish a dog when offered as the animal's exclusive diet. When of a high-quality, premium variety, it is simple to feed and transport, it is relatively odor-free, and it produces firm feces that are easy to pick up and dispose of. As an added bonus, the hard consistency of dry foods, while no substitute for regular veterinary dental cleanings, can help keep the dog's teeth clean between home dental care and cleaning sessions.

Semimoist foods are not typically recommended by breeders and veterinarians as the optimum choice because they can contain colorings and additives that a dog doesn't need, plus

Homecooking for Dogs

Many a dog owner has harbored the romantic notion that it would be oh-so-wonderful to whip up sumptuous, albeit healthy, meals for the family pet each day to ensure that he remains happy and healthy for many years to come. Most of these individuals soon discover, however, that this is a far greater task than it seems, and—wisely—decide to take advantage instead of one of the many complete and balanced diets available on the shelves of the local pet supply store.

If you still feel compelled to cook for your pet, try making some homemade treats instead—perhaps baked dog biscuits in cute canine-oriented shapes—which can be fun and far less demanding. Entire cookbooks exist that feature healthy dog treats fit for the most discriminating canine palate.

their soft texture offers no therapeutic value to the maintenance of the dog's teeth. This latter point could also be made about traditional canned dog foods, but canned foods do tend to find favor among owners who like to make their dogs' dry kibble a bit more appetizing by mixing canned food with the dry for a tasty meal. When the bulk of the diet is comprised of canned food, however, its odor can be offensive should the dog leave some behind after mealtime, and it makes softer, difficult-to-clean stools.

Special Needs, Special Foods

Just as the quality of commercial dog foods has made leaps and bounds in past years, so have the choices expanded significantly. Today, there are foods for every canine need available

at pet supply stores, grocery stores, veterinary offices, and feed stores.

Puppies

Within its first year or so of life, the young Alaskan Malamute could gain 60, 70, even 80 pounds (27, 32, 36 kg) as he travels down that arduous path toward adulthood. Not only will growth occur at a rate that seems almost supernatural, but your dog will also play vigorously during his waking hours. He will therefore require more energy than will the adult Malamute who acts as world class companion rather than world class growing adolescent.

To nourish this hungry puppy, feed the youngster a complete and balanced puppy food that should comprise the bulk of his diet until he reaches 18 months or even two years of age. Don't fall into the trap, however, of believing that this large puppy requires mega-doses of nutrients. That philosophy can lead to bone disease, a common problem in overnourished large-breed puppies that are encouraged nutritionally to grow faster than they should. You must also not allow adult dogs in the house to share the puppy's rations. They will end up overnourished and possibly overweight, which isn't good for any dog.

Older Dogs/Overweight Dogs

Special foods directed toward both older and overweight dogs contain less fat and thus less energy than do regular canine maintenance diets. A food with less fat but sufficient bulk and flavor can help an overweight dog lose some of that weight and prevent a svelte senior citizen from putting on pounds that will tax his aging system. Foods for older dogs also contain less protein, the assumption being that a decrease in protein will reduce strain on the dog's kidneys. Should you decide to switch your dog to a geriatric diet, you may start as early as seven years of age. Should you decide your pup is overweight and needs a low-calorie, low-fat ration, start today.

Active Dogs

A Malamute who takes daily walks or runs with his owner, or who occasionally accompanies the family on day hikes or backpacking trips, can fare just fine on a high-quality canine maintenance diet. But dogs whose days include rigorous athletic conditioning for such activities as pulling a sled, weight pulling, or skijoring (see page 88), may require an extra boost of energy and nutrients. (The same is true of a pregnant or lactating female for whom there are also special diets.) This dog is the ideal candidate for one of the high-energy diets now available.

The owner of such a dog, however, is wise to heed an important lesson from the Arctic people who would reduce their dogs' rations during the summer when their energy needs were not as high as they were in the winter. In other words, during the winter, if your Malamute is a gainfully employed sled dog, increase the daily ration and make sure it meets all of the dog's needs. Then, after the spring thaw, assuming you have not substituted sledding with some other activity of equal physical demands, cut back on the ration to prevent the pitfalls of overnutrition. You may even find that the dog cuts back, reading his own internal signals about what he does and does not need nutritionally.

Ailing Dogs

Dogs with kidney problems, dogs with allergies, dogs with digestive ailments—today there is a broad spectrum of diets available to help

WORDS OF WISDOM

After your dog eats a large meal, keep an eye on him to make sure he does not begin to exhibit signs of canine bloat that could require immediate veterinary attention.

dogs, through nutritional means, deal with the troubles that threaten their health. The very existence of these so-called prescription diets, so named because they are available only from veterinarians, is a testament to how far we have come in our respect for nutrition in our dogs' lives and the valuable tool it provides us in maintaining our pets' health.

Feeding Strategies

How you feed your dog can be just as important as *what* you feed him. For the most part, Malamutes, natural dogs that they are, are considered easy keepers, their evolution in the Arctic having molded their metabolisms into efficient systems that will typically thrive on less food than one might expect for so large a dog. The daily ration for the Malamute, however, will depend on the individual dog, and it can vary anywhere from two cups of dry food a day to six. You can learn where in this range your dog falls by paying close attention to his eating habits, gauging his weight and conformation, and consulting with the dog's breeder and veterinarian.

In addition to determining *how much* your dog should be eating is the question of *how* to feed your pet. It seems so simple, yet opinions vary widely on this. The best option for a particular owner and a particular dog usually depends on which strategy meshes with the

Canine athletes, such as this sled team of Malamutes, often require a diet higher in fats and carbohydrates to fuel their energy needs.

owner's lifestyle and schedule and is more comfortable for the dog.

A popular choice is feeding the dog his entire ration in one daily feeding. This is convenient for the owner who may not be home during the day to split the daily ration into two or three smaller feedings, but the once-a-day regimen won't work for every Malamute. Puppies, for example, cannot be fed once a day because their energy needs are enormous as they experience rapid growth that requires constant infusions of fuel.

Two or three feedings a day will better sustain a puppy, and is also the wisest choice for dogs that may be prone to canine bloat (gastric dilitation-volvulus). Bloat is common among large dogs and dogs that tend to wolf down large meals, so dividing the daily ration into several feedings can help prevent this deadly condition.

Avoiding Poor Eating Habits

Nutrition is a powerful tool at every dog owner's disposal. With that tool you can enhance your pet's health and comfort, and possibly add years to his life, as well.

But powerful tools can have a down side, too. Where there are great benefits to be reaped on one side of the equation, there can also be great danger on the other side. As we have seen, dog foods have come a long way in the last few decades, offering our pets carefully formulated nutrition designed to fuel their various nutritional needs, but at the same time, we are also seeing an epidemic of obesity in dogs, and the two trends walk hand in hand.

Obesity

Obesity is a sad state for a dog (or human!). The dog may genuinely enjoy wolfing down the leftovers from each family member's dinner plate, and may genuinely relish receiving his own bowl of ice cream for dessert, but to allow the dog to grow accustomed to such habits is not doing the animal any favors. Aside from the fact that poor nutrition takes a terrible toll on internal organs, an obese dog simply is not comfortable. He cannot run and play as he should, his breathing comes hard, and his movements are slow and labored. Worse yet, in allowing a dog to become obese, owners are ensuring that their days with a beloved family member will be substantially reduced. Is it worth it?

If you are unsure about whether your dog is overweight (not always easy with a thick-coated Malamute), try this test: With your dog in a standing position, run your hands down his rib cage. Do you feel the ribs? If not, it's time for a diet.

Fortunately, with the new weight reducing dog foods, you need not starve a dog to help him take off those extra pounds. In most cases, the success of a canine weight-loss program involves the owner's resolve more than the dog's. The dog's human family members—all of them—must learn to say "No" to those big brown eyes begging scraps from the table. They must bid farewell to their own bad "treating" habits, and help build new, healthier eating and exercise habits in their pet.

The Underweight Malamute

If you do the obesity rib test and do feel ribs, you should think about that result as well. Are the ribs sharp and overly defined, or do you just feel the outline of the bones as well as some surrounding tissue? If the latter is true, your dog is just right. If the former is the case, your dog is probably in need of a bit more fat and calories, but these must be offered via dog food and the doctor's orders, not by what you have left over on the dinner table each night.

If yours is a thin dog, he may be a so-called finicky eater, but don't let this send you rushing to the pet store to stock up on every type of dog food and treat to entice your pet to the food dish. Stick with one food and avoid not only digestive upset in your dog, but finicky eating habits, as well.

Treats

Finally, whether your dog is overweight, underweight, or just right, take it easy with the

WORDS OF WISDOM

In addition to the rib test to gauge your dog's weight status, you can also try the eye test. In other words, look at your big beautiful Malamute and see if he has a waistline. Look at him from the side and from the top, and determine whether, under all that hair, his lower back and abdomen area nip in a bit before the base of his powerful hindquarters. If you see the broad shoulders and rib cage taper back into the curve of a waist rather than remain a boxy, uniform physique from rib cage to tail, your dog is probably just right. If not, well, perhaps a bit more exercise and a reduction of treats are in order.

treats. An overweight dog may have to cut out the usual treats, but may find he enjoys substitute carrot or zucchini slices instead. During the holidays, you may look forward to preparing a plate of turkey, stuffing, mashed potatoes, and gravy for your pet to make for a truly memorable celebration. You may end up, however, remembering not the meal, but the fact that you had to stay up all night cleaning up the dog's diarrhea.

Instead, pop open a can of turkey dog food and offer that instead. The dog that is accustomed to dry food will consider this a grand treat, while you remain guilt-free. And skip the dessert. Such foods have absolutely no place in the canine diet—especially true of chocolate, which is poisonous gastrointestinally to dogs because of an ingredient theobromine. Train yourself to stick to these few rules, and you increase the odds that your dog will remain by your side for many years to come.

GROOMING: THE MALAMUTE BEAUTIFUL

While it takes a special brand of individual to live successfully with the Alaskan Malamute, it doesn't take much to keep that old soul looking her best. Indeed, the Arctic people who first lived with this dog were too busy to spend much time making sure that their dogs were well groomed, so fortunately for them—and today for us—this very natural breed comes graced with a coat that demands little in the way of extraordinary care.

Understanding the Coat

It would be a terrible mistake to suggest that the Malamute need not be groomed or that she may be neglected and will in turn radiate as a beautiful dog. Rather, the Malamute should be groomed on a regular basis, and the more regularly this is pursued, the easier it will be to accomplish.

The first step toward grooming the Alaskan Malamute is to understand that all care in this department revolves around the dog's thick

The beauty and loyalty of the Alaskan Malamute has been known to warm the hearts of those privileged to live with and care for this dog.

double coat, the unifying signature of every breed within the family of Nordic dogs. This coat is truly a miraculous feat of Mother Nature's engineering, embodying, as the name implies, two distinctly different coats that work together to create a dynamic, and extremely effective, whole.

Bury your fingers into the coat of a Malamute, and you will get a feel for both coats. Your fingers are first greeted by long, coarse guard hairs that may even seem a bit stiffer than you are accustomed to feeling on most dogs. Dig in deeper, down to the skin, and there you will find a new sensation, your fingers suddenly coming to rest on a bed of soft, downlike fluff—the undercoat. Through this

A complete head-to-toe brushing of an Alaskan Malamute can be a rigorous, time-consuming job, but you need not complete the entire task in a single grooming session. Once you have trained your Malamute to accept and enjoy the thorough brushing of her lovely coat, concentrate on one section of her body per session. Choose, say, the front right side, lay your dog down on her side, and concentrate all your efforts on brushing and combing the chosen section down to the skin. Not only will you be treating your pup like a princess at a spa, but in the course of a few days, you will have successfully and thoroughly tended to every inch of hair and skin on her body.

simple act, you have just discovered why this breed has so successfully thrived in some of the most extremely frigid climates and conditions this planet has to offer. It's all in the coat.

Working together, the dog's outer guard hairs and soft, fluffy undercoat are able to trap air close to the dog's body and warm the air with her own body heat. As dense as the coat is—and assuming the dog has not fallen through the ice into a freezing body of water—the coat is also able to keep dangerous moisture at bay. As moisture from ice, snow, or rain clings to the outermost tips of the guard hairs, it is unable to slide down toward the undercoat where it might saturate that soft fluff and then the skin, thus chilling and potentially killing the dog in freezing temperatures. As testament to this system's efficacy, you have likely seen photographs of Arctic sled dogs curled up in the snow, their coats powdered white as if dusted with confectioners' sugar, the dogs slumbering peacefully, warm and dry within their protective outer shells.

Care of the Double Coat

Needless to say, helping the Malamute care for this mantle of hair, a coat that also tends not to convey that strong and rather distinctive "doggy" odor prevalent in other breeds, is a big responsibility, but not as daunting as it may seem.

One important key is to start early. The earlier a puppy learns to tolerate grooming and cleanliness, the quicker she will adjust. That will help to keep grooming sessions positive. Whether it is that occasional bath, nail clipping, or routine daily brushing, the dog should look forward to grooming, not dread it. In sharing these moments, you are on one hand reinforcing your position as leader, as the dog must cooperate with you, but you are also enhancing the bond you share with your pet.

Once you make coat and skin care a part of the routine, it will accustom you to what is normal for your pet. You will thus be prepared to recognize immediately if the dog develops abnormal lumps or bumps, or if her skin and coat suddenly become dry or otherwise unhealthy, which could signal an internal health problem.

Unlike breeds that require extensive and frequent grooming to keep their coats healthy and free of mats, the very natural Malamute requires no such heroic attentions. She rarely needs a bath, and haircuts are unnecessary. What she does require is an owner who enjoys brushing his or her dog on a regular basis, which can be time consuming but does not require any unattainable level of specialized skill or training.

Time spent outdoors can make the grooming of your Malamute even more of a challenge.

Supplies and Techniques for Coat Care

The supplies you gather for this job may vary. Some breeders and owners use the pin brush, an oval-shaped brush with thick, metal bristles that resemble heads of pins, while others swear by the slicker, a rectangular field of fine metal bristles that can effectively remove dead hair (although some believe it also breaks the hair left behind). Regardless of the type of brush you choose, thoroughness is everything.

Sure it's simple just to run a brush superficially through the dog's hair on her back and leave it at that, but in doing so you will not address the needs of the undercoat, or, even more importantly, reach the skin, which requires stimulation both for proper circulation and for the distribution of healthy coat oils. A more effective method of brushing and removing dead hair involves first brushing against the grain of the hair, brushing against the direction in which the guard hairs tend to lie. This way you automatically brush the undercoat and the guard hairs simultaneously, while reaching the skin as well. When this job is done, then you may brush with the growth of the hair for a polished, finished look. Brush the dog this way anywhere from three times a week to once a day, and you will find yourself with a Malamute that can't help but command attention.

You must be careful to brush the more difficult-to-reach spots, as well, to prevent mats that must be cut out should they develop. Don't forget that hidden region under the front leg (under the elbow), and pay close attention to the haunches, the underbelly, and that soft area behind the ears, all areas that can become riddled with mats if ignored.

The rake: Another tool Malamute veterans recommend is the rake. This comes in handy particularly once or twice a year when the Malamute sheds its soft, fluffy undercoat, a

process referred to as "blowing coat." The old coat, having performed its duties well, sheds out to make room for the growth of a newer, fresher growth of hair. The rake can help speed up this process, as can a weekly bath until the coat is fully shed.

Bathtime Made Easier

Without a doubt, the simplest way to bathe your dog is to have the job done by a professional groomer. Grooming shops are outfitted with all the right equipment that makes grooming so large a dog convenient or even possible. But, with a little planning, you can adapt similar techniques to accommodate your dog at home, and thus gain an immense sense of accomplishment from bathing this beautiful animal yourself. The following steps should help you in this mission.

Prepare for the Big Event

Before you even think of rounding up your dog for a bath, you must prepare. First, determine where you will be bathing the dog. This is actually possible in your own bathtub with a rubber mat on the bottom if you don't mind cleaning the bathroom from floor to ceiling afterward, but it may also be done outdoors (on a warm day, of course) in a child's wading pool, a metal washtub, or just out on the grass or patio with a hose and the dog tied to a sturdy anchor. Prepare the site ahead of time, filling the tub with lukewarm water, hooking up the hose, whatever you need to do to accommodate your water needs.

Introduce grooming procedures to a young puppy in a positive manner, and she will be more inclined to accept them as an adult.

Now gather your supplies. You will need:

- ✔ several clean, dry towels
- ✔ a shampoo formulated for dogs (perhaps a flea shampoo or one that also includes a conditioner)
- ✔ a couple of clean washcloths
- ✔ a large plastic cup to assist in rinsing
- ✔ a blow dryer (optional)

Place these all near the tub and you're ready to begin.

Splish, Splash

Because this breed is so adept at reading minds, your Malamute will probably guess before you even make a move that you intend to give her a bath. She may try to avoid you, to stay just out of reach or perhaps to disappear. Whatever you must contend with, retrieve the dog and bring her to the bath. Your first challenge is to wet the dog from head to toe (or perhaps from neck to toe, some dogs being more amenable to the bath if their heads and faces can remain dry until the end). This can be a challenge because that thick double coat will fight full saturation. Spend as much time as you can in accomplishing this, and you will find the rest of the bath proceeds much more smoothly.

Now, faced with a wet dog, begin the shampooing. Just as you attempted to wet the coat down to the skin, now you will try to massage the shampoo through the hair and down to the skin, as well. In doing so, don't neglect the areas beneath the tail, the groin, behind the ears, and the profuse growth of hair at the bottom of the dog's feet.

Once the dog is sufficiently cleansed, it's time to rinse. This time it's even more critical to saturate the dog completely as you must remove every bit of soap from the dog's skin and hair.

Thorough weekly brushings are usually all the Malamute requires to keep its thick double coat healthy (except once or twice a year when the undercoat "blows," at which time the dog requires daily attention to keep the shedding under control).

Rinse from the top of the neck and back and work your way down to the legs and feet. Then rinse, rinse, rinse again. When you no longer see soap or bubbles falling from the dog, rinse one more time. If you have reserved the washing of the dog's face and head for the end, wash the head with a drop of shampoo, the face with a clean washcloth and water, and you have successfully completed the bath.

Proper Drying

Equally important to the rinse cycle is the drying of the dog. To prevent the animal from becoming chilled, you will want to make sure she is completely dry before she runs off to resume her normal activities.

To tackle the drying of that thick double coat, begin by first patting and rubbing the dog with clean towels. Once the bulk of the water has been dried or shaken off, confine the dog in a warm dry spot, perhaps a corner of the kitchen, the garage, or a sheltered area outdoors to finish drying. You can accelerate the process by using a blow dryer set on warm, not hot, blowing the hair dry by directing the air against the lay of the coat (so as to dry the undercoat as well). Because the noise and sensation may startle some dogs, it is wise to introduce your pet to the blow dryer at a young age, allowing her first to explore the dryer as it sits unplugged on the floor, then introducing her to its sound, and then to the

The clean, well-groomed Malamute is nothing short of breathtaking.

feel of the air on her coat. Most dogs, when introduced to it properly and positively, learn to enjoy being dried with the blow dryer, which can certainly help to ensure that the dog is dried all the way down to the skin.

Fighting Fleas and Ticks

Fleas

No discussion of dog grooming would be complete without mention of the seemingly neverending fight against external parasites, particularly the fight against the flea. Millions of dollars are spent each year on flea products, evidence of just how prevalent this problem can be in households where dogs reside.

The key to combating this parasite, two of which can become millions in a blink of an eye, is to launch your offense on three fronts: The dog, the house, and the yard. If you find one flea on your dog, then rest assured that your entire house and yard have been infiltrated by adult fleas and flea eggs and larvae as well. All must be targeted.

The dog: Begin with the dog, treating her with effective yet safe flea products, perhaps a combination of bath, dip, and spray (all of which must be compatible with each other to prevent a toxic reaction; consult your dog's veterinarian for advice on mixing and matching).

The dog world has in recent years experienced a revolution in the area of flea control. This is found in the rise of flea-control products that now allow us to fight the little bloodsuckers from the inside out.

These products include the insect growth regulators, which are typically administered orally each month, and inhibit the development of flea eggs and larvae so they may never reach adulthood and indulge their kind's thirst for blood. Also available are the so-called "adulticides," which are typically administered on the skin at the dog's shoulder blades and make their way into the animal's system, where they work to kill adult fleas that have the audacity to bite into an unsuspecting host.

The home: While the dog is being defleaed and treated, attack the household as well. A variety of sprays and bombs are available that will destroy both adult and preadult (eggs and larvae) fleas that may be hiding in the carpet, the furniture, your dog's bed, your bed, etc.

The yard: Finally, give the same attention to the yard, for here you will find fleas and their families just waiting to hitch a ride on the family pet for an entry into the house.

The warmer months of the year are typically the time when fleas are the greatest problem, so for most owners, this is a seasonal battle. In some areas where the weather remains balmy most of the time, it rages year round. Either way, success requires an owner who is willing to commit to the three-pronged attack on a routine basis.

Discuss all product options and your entire flea-control program with your dog's veterinarian to determine how best to address flea colonization on your Malamute. With such a powerful arsenal at your disposal, it is best to follow the veterinarian's advice rather than devise your own game plan, and remember that products appropriate for adult dogs may be too toxic for youngsters.

A Malamute poses for the camera.

Ticks

When you declare war on fleas, as an added bonus you may be targeting ticks, as well, for the products that destroy the former often do the same to the latter. Whether or not your flea-control products target ticks as well, check your dog's skin and coat carefully from head to toe every time you return from a foray into tick country, just to be sure.

If you should find a tick on your dog's skin, you cannot simply brush it away as you would a fly. Grasp the body of the tick and as much of its head as possible firmly between your thumb and forefinger (if possible wear latex gloves), and pull it out slowly with a sure, steady movement. Apply a topical antibiotic ointment to the site to prevent infection, and watch the dog for several weeks to make sure she does not begin to exhibit signs of illness, stiffness, or lethargy.

Just as you must care for the Malamute's coat on a routine basis, the ears, eyes, feet, and teeth also require some attention. Maintain them now when they are healthy, and you'll prevent problems down the line.

Ear Care

The Malamute boasts an acute hearing ability, evident in the shape of her ears. The breed is fortunate in that its prick ears are not typically candidates for the problems and infections that can affect floppy-eared dogs. The following tips will help keep them that way:

✔ Look inside the ears periodically to ensure they remain clean, and, more importantly, smell them. Get to know what your dog's healthy ear smells

Clean your Malamute's ear with a clean cotton ball dipped in mineral oil. Clean only the ear flap and avoid the delicate ear canal.

like so you will be able to detect an abnormal odor should one ever develop.

✔ To clean your dog's ears, resist the temptation to stick cotton swabs or similarly dangerous objects into the ear canal. Keep to the open, visible ear flaps, cleaning them occasionally with mineral oil on a cotton ball.

✔ If, during the routine care of the ears, you come to suspect a problem—or if you notice your dog scratching incessantly at one ear or shaking her head violently—contact the veterinarian.

Eye Care

Like the Malamute's ears, her eyes, too, should require little care, yet remain vigilant in your observations and observe the following protocols:

✔ Become familiar with what the dog's eyes normally look like so you will be able to detect such abnormalities as an unusual cast to the cornea or a sudden increase in tearing.

✔ Clean the corners of the dog's eyes as needed with a damp washcloth. If the eyes appear red or irritated, do not treat them with drops or medications meant for humans unless instructed by the veterinarian to do so.

✔ Should you notice a sudden change in the eyes, consult the veterinarian. Sometimes a simple pollen allergy can be the cause of tearing, but don't rely on do-it-yourself diagnosis and treatment. The eyes are too important for shortcuts, and sometimes serious problems elsewhere in the body manifest secondarily as changes in the eye.

Foot Care

The typical Malamute has large feet with an abundant growth of hair around the paw pads. Since feet are the foundation of athletic movement, don't neglect them as key targets of the grooming regimen:

✔ While conformation show exhibitors may trim the hair around the edge of the feet to refine their look, the pet Malamute should require no such grooming.

✔ Check the feet regularly to make sure that the thick growth of hair remains free of ice, balls of snow, salt, and mud, and that the delicate skin between the toes does not become impaled by foxtails.

✔ Examine and clean the feet carefully after any outdoor adventure; you never know what your Malamute might pick up as she runs through the snow or explores a mountain trail.

Nail Care

Most dogs don't enjoy having their nails trimmed but they should be taught, preferably as puppies, to tolerate it.

✔ Trim the dog's nails on a regular basis, as overgrown nails can cause pain, limping, and even infection. Depending on the dog, the nails may require trimming anywhere from every two weeks to once a month.

✔ Don't allow the nails to grow to the point where the toes begin to curl up when the dog stands. If your dog has her dewclaws—the nails up on the ankle that don't touch the ground and are often removed from young puppies— remember that they must be trimmed too.

✔ When trimming the nails, avoid the quick, the blood-rich base of the nail. With a pair of quality nail clippers designed especially for large dogs, clip only the tip of the nail and avoid the region where it darkens.

✔ If you do "quick" the dog, the nail will bleed profusely, so be prepared. Apply either special blood-stopping powder or a styptic pencil, both of which are available at pet supply stores. Have these supplies ready, because even the most skilled nail trimmer has been known to cut just a little too far down from time to time.

Tooth Care

With dogs now living longer than ever before, great demands are being placed on their teeth that would have been moot for dogs, say, 30 years ago. Back then, dogs only needed their teeth for eight, nine, maybe ten years, as that tended to be the average canine lifespan. There really was no such thing as canine gum disease,

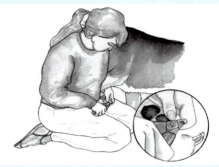

The dog will look upon nail clipping positively if you introduce her to the procedure at a young age, and take great care not to cut the sensitive, blood-rich quick at the base of the nail.

and little thought was given to the fact that dogs could develop cavities (the latter of which are more rare in dogs than is the former). Now all that has changed, and diligent owners are wise to do all they can to help their dogs keep their teeth into their senior years. The following guidelines can assist you in this mission:

✔ Have the dog's teeth professionally cleaned by a veterinarian once or twice a year. Supplement this with brushing at home, ideally every day, but at least two or three times a week.

✔ Brush your dog's teeth with a toothbrush and toothpaste specially designed for dogs (human toothpastes can cause digestive upset in dogs). These items are available at pet supply stores, as are alternatives such as finger brushes and specially coated gauze pads, which may be used on puppies or adult dogs that don't care to cooperate with traditional brushing.

✔ To brush your dog's teeth, proceed just as you would to brush your own teeth. To reach the molars in back, if the dog is amenable, place your finger into the corner of her lips and pull back gently to expose the molars for brushing.

THE PICTURE OF HEALTH

Nothing is more stunning than a beautiful Alaskan Malamute with a clean, lustrous double coat; clear, alert eyes; a well-muscled physique; and an aura of stamina molded by centuries of existence in some of the most frigid regions of the globe. This vision of canine beauty is the Malamute's legacy, but it is not achieved without some effort on the part of the owner.

The Veterinary Partnership

While the fostering of the Malamute's health and well-being begins at home, its continued success relies on the partnership between the dog's owner and his veterinarian. The owner depends on the veterinarian to provide the dog with both routine preventive care and the treatments required for injuries and illness, and the veterinarian relies on the owner's vigilant observations and knowledge of the dog so that he or she can in turn offer the most effective treatment possible.

Selecting the ideal veterinarian is a great responsibility. While this alone can be daunting, so is the cost of proper veterinary care. However, this is an element of Malamute ownership that should be considered long before the animal ever joins the household.

The maintenance of your Malamute's health and well-being are key to his longevity.

Several avenues exist for choosing your dog's veterinarian. First, ask for recommendations from other dog owners, from your dog's breeder, or even from local animal shelter personnel, all of whom will be well acquainted with the veterinarians in your area and their individual philosophies toward their vocation.

One visit will usually give you a good indication as to whether you and your dog are compatible with a particular practitioner. Observe carefully how the doctor interacts with your dog. Does your dog seem comfortable around this individual? Do you feel free to ask questions, which are then answered clearly and concisely?

Take this opportunity to ask about specific concerns you might have for the future care of your pet. For example, how are off-hours emergencies handled? Will the doctor refer you to specialists, such as an ophthalmologist or orthopedist?

Get to know your dog when he is healthy, and you will recognize immediately the signs that indicate illness or injury.

━━━━━━ **TIP** ━━━━━━

Classic Canine Warning Signs
   Should your dog exhibit any of the following potential signs of illness, consult his veterinarian:
- Loss of appetite
- Excessive vomiting
- Diarrhea, especially if it is tinged with blood
- Loss of quality of haircoat, hair loss, and dry skin
- Incessant shaking of the head
- Skin lumps and bumps
- Constipation or difficulty urinating
- Unexplained and/or rapid weight loss or weight gain
- Uncharacteristic listlessness or lethargy
- Limping
- Foul odor from the ear
- Watering eyes

In making these all-important evaluations, remember you are not beholden to remain with a veterinarian simply because he or she has treated your dog once or twice or even for a year or two. If you are for any reason dissatisfied, keep looking. Your pet should enjoy many years of health and contentment, and through those years you want to work with a veterinarian who will not only see the dog through his many stages of life, but who will also make both you and your pet feel comfortable with every visit.

A Keen Eye

   In addition to choosing a veterinarian, the most critical step toward optimum health care of an Alaskan Malamute—or of any dog—is preventive care. The owner should take the responsibility seriously of taking the dog to the veterinarian for important routine checkups and vaccinations.

   The same diligence must apply to the owner's care and observations of the dog at home. In virtually every potential health problem that can affect a beloved pet, from parvovirus to heartworm to cancer, early diagnosis is key to the dog's recovery and even survival. If you know your dog well when he is healthy, you will be better prepared to recognize immediately when things just aren't right.

Dogs cannot tell the doctor what is ailing them. Sometimes a veterinarian's ability even to determine where it hurts can be a challenge. But there are telltale signs that indicate that all is not right with the animal, and the observant owner can recognize these signs quickly and easily, ideally in the earliest stages of an illness' progression.

Early Signs of Illness

The classic signs of illness in a dog can be fairly standard from illness to illness. Diarrhea, vomiting, and a loss of appetite, for example, are not illnesses in and of themselves, but rather *signs* of illness that obviously deviate from what is normal for the healthy dog. These three symptoms in particular can mean something as minor as a simple gastric upset, or something as critical as a case of parvovirus, and often only the veterinarian can determine the cause.

The sudden development of a limp could indicate joint problems or the onset of hip dysplasia; the incessant shaking of the head is the classic sign of an ear infection or embedded foxtail; or even a dog's drastic change in behavior, such as a typically gregarious dog suddenly becoming lethargic, are all signals that should send the owner to the veterinarian. Malamutes tend to be linked quite closely to their owners and are usually more than willing to let them know as best they can that something just isn't right. It is then up to the dog's owner to heed those signals and act accordingly.

Even if the dog is showing no signs of illness or unusual behavior, keep your eyes open and make home examinations part of the daily, or at least weekly, care routine. Do some hands-on work as well. During grooming, examine both coat and skin for changes in texture or landscape. Smell the ears for strange odors or a change in their normal scents. Take a look at the groin for lumps, bumps, or anything else that might be unusual there. Pay attention to the dog's frequency and ease of urination and bowel movements. This will prepare you to recognize abnormal signs should they emerge later on.

Magic in a Syringe

Some of the most important players in the preventive medical care of the Alaskan Malamute are the dog's routine vaccinations. Thanks to advancements in the veterinary care of companion animals, we now have access to a variety of vaccines that protect our pets from illnesses that at one time ran rampant and spelled certain death for the unfortunate animals that contracted them.

These vaccinations, which typically begin during puppyhood, involve a series administered over several months' time. During the first weeks of life a puppy is protected by the maternal antibodies he receives from his mother's milk. After weaning, those antibodies can remain in the pup's system, rendering his vaccinations impotent. Thus only a series of vaccinations can help guarantee full protection in the long run.

WORDS OF WISDOM

The rabies vaccine, which protects a dog from a fatal disease and is required by law nationwide, is critical for any dog, but is particularly critical for a dog as outdoorsy in nature as the Alaskan Malamute. He may encounter such rabies-prone animals as skunks and raccoons that trigger his predatory nature leading to a chase and an unhappy ending.

Consult your veterinarian for advice on a vaccination schedule that is appropriate for your puppy.

The Vaccine Debate

A few years back, new puppy owners would bring their new addition and cart him off to the veterinarian's office to begin a series of vaccines targeting various canine illnesses. This original series of three or four injections would then be followed by annual boosters for the rest of the dog's life. In recent years, however, critics of the accepted traditional program—veterinarians and laypeople alike—have come to believe that perhaps a one-size-fits-all approach is not necessarily the best prescription for every dog.

Some vaccines are and should be mandated by public policy (rabies comes to mind). Others target such severe and/or highly contagious illnesses—distemper, parvovirus, and tracheo-bronchitis (formerly known as kennel cough)—for which routine vaccinations are required before dogs can enter boarding kennels, partici-pate in training classes and other canine activi-ties, or travel the dog-show circuit. But more and more dog owners these days are finding veterinarians who are willing to design custom vaccine schedules for their patients, basing the particular vaccines and their frequency on a dog's lifestyle and home region.

For example, the Lyme disease vaccine is probably best suited to a dog who frequently traverses wooded areas that disease-carrying deer ticks call home. Or perhaps a veterinarian will determine that the leptospirosis vaccine is unnecessary for dogs in a particular area where that disease is never found. As for frequency, practitioners and their owners may decide to supplement the custom vaccine schedule with periodic blood tests performed on the dog to monitor the status of his immunity. The results of those tests can then guide the need, or lack thereof, for boosters. Those who follow such game plans do so out of a desire to ensure that their dogs remain protected while minimizing the administration of unnecessary vaccines.

The Case for Spaying and Neutering

The results are in and they are indisputable. The altered dog, whether it is the spayed female or the neutered male, is generally healthier and longer lived than its intact counterpart, and it is likely to be a far superior pet. On the health

The Breeding Question

It is difficult to imagine someone taking the breeding of Malamutes lightly, but this happens far too often in the dog world, much to the detriment of the breed in question. In the Malamute's case, this has led to the development of such genetic problems as hip dysplasia, night blindness, dwarfism, and hypothyroidism.

Considering the serious repercussions of casual breeding, one should not breed a dog based on misguided notions that there are profits to be made from doing so. Stud fees, prenatal veterinary visits for mom, plus the proper everyday care of the family will quickly eat up any profits one imagines are inherent in this endeavor. Nor should a parental desire for a child to experience "the miracle of life" be the motivation. Not only is this unfair to the pup-

pies, but it also neglects the fact that much can go wrong in the whelping of puppies, especially when it is done casually, and you may end up with a litter of orphaned pups who require 24-hour care if they are to survive.

In addition, the well-meaning family that seeks to breed the family dog as a biology lesson, or because they believe their darling pet should have "just one litter" before she is spayed, too often end up giving the resulting puppies away to unsuitable homes out of desperation, or turning them over to the animal shelter when they discover there really aren't enough homes out there after all—especially for dogs that could soon weigh 100 pounds (45.4 kg) or more. This is not generally the message parents seek to impart to their children about the responsibilities of pet care.

front, the altered female, especially when she is spayed during puppyhood, is less prone to such maladies as mammary cancer and the various infections unique to the uterus and related organs. The same is true of the neutered male, which, after this very routine procedure, is far less likely to contract such illnesses as anal tumors and testicular cancer.

Spaying and neutering provide mental health benefits as well. Malamute owners, for example, typically find that altering this particular breed can make so large an animal easier to handle. This is not to say that the procedures in any way diminish the dog's energy levels or make the animal any less of an athlete or exercise companion. Rather, the altered Malamute is less

likely to roam, as such behavior is typically linked to a search for a mate, and he is more attuned to his owner than to the activities and scents of others of his own kind. Isn't that why we choose to live with dogs in the first place?

Nevertheless, despite the great benefits of spaying and neutering, which should override any emotional human responses, the myths persist. We hear altered dogs are fat. Altered dogs are lazy. Not so. Weight gain and lethargy are products of an owner's inattention to a dog's exercise needs and a propensity to overfeed, both of which have nothing to do with the animal's ability or inability to reproduce.

And finally, spaying and neutering bring the dual reward of being socially responsible. With so many dogs, including purebred Alaskan Malamutes, ending up in shelters and with rescue groups each year, you can ensure that your pet will never contribute to that problem.

Common Canine Ailments

Even with the most vigilant preventive care, illness is usually inevitable at one time or another during the long life of your beloved pet. The following are a few conditions to watch for, and to act on, as soon as any suspicious symptoms raise their ugly heads.

Bloat

A profound veterinary emergency, bloat, also known as gastric dilitation-volvulus, occurs when a buildup of gas and/or fluid accumulates in a dog's stomach, which may then rotate, block off any chance of that buildup dissipating, and thus constrict the dog's circulatory system.

A dog suffering from bloat will exhibit signs of restlessness and abdominal pain; his stomach

A solid program of preventive veterinary care, which includes annual checkups, can help a dog live well into its teens.

will swell and he will salivate excessively and unsuccessfully attempt to vomit or defecate. As the condition progresses, and if the stomach twists, the dog will go into shock. Without immediate veterinary attention, which may include surgery to turn and anchor the stomach into the proper position, the dog can die.

As a member of the larger family of dogs, Malamutes are prone to canine bloat that, though it can affect any dog, typically targets larger animals as its victims. There are measures an owner can take to prevent it. Because its occurrence is directly linked to eating habits, Malamute owners should prevent their pets from gulping their food and from drinking large amounts of water after eating, habits common in multidog households, where dogs may believe they must eat quickly or lose their food to another dog. In such households, dogs should be fed separately and in individual dishes.

Of equal value is feeding pets several small meals throughout the day rather than one large meal, and preventing dogs from exercising vigorously right after eating.

Heartworm Disease

Heartworm disease is a devastating illness transmitted by mosquitoes, which is caused by a worm that settles in the dog's heart and ultimately kills its host. Treatment can be long and traumatic and prove almost as dangerous to the dog as does the infestation of the heartworms themselves.

Given the severity of this disease, it is worth your while to protect your pet from this devastating illness, and it is indeed fortunate that this can be done effectively with veterinary assistance. This begins with a blood test to determine that the dog is clear of infestation, followed by the administration once a month of a prescription preventive that will protect the dog from the disease. As an added bonus, many heartworm preventives target other internal parasites as well.

Heatstroke

If you leave your Malamute in the car during summer, allow him to overexert himself in the heat, or confine him to an area of direct sunlight with no shade or water, you are asking for trouble. Within minutes, the temperature within that hot car, for instance, even with the windows down and a shady parking spot, can climb to well over 100°F (37.8°C). The dog's normal body temperature of 101 to 102°F can skyrocket right along with it in an equally short period of time.

Dogs in general have a very low tolerance for heat, their only mechanism for cooling their bodies being the panting reflex, which is not all that effective. A dog afflicted with heatstroke will pant frantically, salivate profusely, perhaps stagger and vomit, and ultimately lapse into a coma that, without treatment, will lead to death. Treatment involves a gradual cooling of the animal with a bath or hose-down of cool (not cold) water, and a move to a cooler, shadier, preferably air-conditioned, environment.

The goal is to lower the animal's body temperature to 103°F (39°C), and many cases do require an emergency trip to the veterinarian to ensure that the condition is properly halted and reversed. Because such efforts are not always successful, a better alternative is prevention.

Hereditary Disorders

Like all pure breeds of dogs, the Alaskan Malamute is prone to several genetic problems. Most of these, however, can be avoided by pur-

A commitment to lifelong learning and companionship is the greatest gift you can offer your dog.

chasing a dog or puppy only from parents that have tested clear of the conditions, and by refusing to breed a dog that has such problems either itself or in its background.

Hip dysplasia is one such condition. While it may occur in various degrees of severity, hip dysplasia typically becomes apparent in a dog by the time he reaches his second birthday. The condition is a potentially crippling deformity of the hips that can affect any dog, but it is most prevalent in large dogs. As it progresses, the affected dog will exhibit increasingly dramatic signs of pain, move stiffly, perhaps limp, and even decline invitations to play and exercise. Treatment, depending on the severity of the condition, may range from pharmaceutical pain management to surgery. The incidence of hip dysplasia is tracked by the Orthopedic Foundation for Animals (OFA). Dogs that test clear after being x-rayed at two years of age are

Early signs of hip dysplasia are stiffness when standing and, possibly, a limp.

considered OFA certified and are the only animals that should be bred.

The OFA also tracks *hypothyroidism,* which is on the increase in Malamutes. In this condition, the most common hormonal affliction of the canine species, a sluggish thyroid gland cannot secrete sufficient amounts of thyroid hormone. This in turn causes the dog to gain weight, grow uncharacteristically lethargic, and perhaps experience hair loss and related skin and coat problems. Once identified, the condition can usually be reversed with hormone replacement therapy, which the patient will probably require for the remainder of his life.

Chondrodysplasia (ChD), also known as dwarfism, is a heartbreaking hereditary condition, in which the affected dog is born with deformed legs that grow increasingly so as he matures. As a recessive condition, both parents must be carriers for their offspring to develop chondrodysplasia, but even a carrier dog that

exhibits no signs should not be bred. To combat the problem, the Alaskan Malamute Club of America has established the Chondrodysplasia Certification Committee to identify affected dogs and carriers, and alert owners and breeders to the dogs that should not be bred. Only by honoring this program can breeders hope to eradicate the condition.

Another condition with a presumed genetic component is coat funk, a mysterious deterioration, discoloration, and loss of hair that occurs in varying levels of severity among mature Malamutes and some other, typically double-coated, breeds. Though some theories hold that coat funk might be related to a malfunction of the endocrine system, the jury is still out on the true root cause and how it might be effectively treated. Malamute enthusiasts are hoping that current research into the condition will begin to reveal some answers in the years to come.

Internal Parasites

While most parasites may not be deadly to an affected dog (unless that dog is quite young), their presence does undermine the dog's overall health and interferes with his optimum quality of life.

Internal parasites, such as the very common roundworms and tapeworms, they make their homes in a dog's intestines, can be easily discovered in the animal's feces, assuming, of course, that the owner is attuned to such necessary unpleasantries. The presence of tapeworms, for example, is easily detectable by the ricelike tapeworm segments that appear in the affected dog's feces or around his anus. As for roundworms, the owner should be willing to bring a fecal sample from his or her pet to the veterinarian twice a year for evaluation. In both cases, the worms can be easily eradicated upon diagnosis with prescription medications. Stick with your veterinarian's diagnosis and treatment plan and steer clear of "quick-fix" over-the-counter remedies that can do more harm than good.

You can further prevent tapeworms, which are transmitted by fleas, by instituting a sound flea control program (see page 62). In the case of other various and sundry intestinal worms, preventing the dog from coming into contact with potentially infested feces of other dogs is the key to keeping your pet's insides parasite-free.

Kennel Cough

So named because it is most often transmitted from dog to dog in kennel situations, kennel cough, or canine infectious tracheobronchitis, is a highly contagious, though not typically serious, condition that affects a dog's respiratory system. One experience with kennel cough—particularly the harsh, honking, dry cough that

Malamute health relies on communication between owner and veterinarian.

can remain with the animal for a week or two or even longer—and it is understandable why owners would want to protect their pets, and themselves, from this ordeal.

Prevention of this illness is simple enough, provided by a vaccine known as *Bordetella,* that may be administered either by injection or through the nostrils. Any dog that is to be kenneled should receive this vaccine (and most kennels mandate that all canine residents be vaccinated), as well as dogs that will be experiencing dog-to-dog contact in show situations, sled dog races, weight pulls, dog parks, or at field trials. When choosing a kennel, it is also wise to go with one that is kept squeaky clean, as cleanliness, too, is directly linked to the spread of kennel cough and other canine ailments.

Parvovirus

Canine parvovirus is a serious viral infection that affects the intestines. Signs of parvovirus are diarrhea (especially diarrhea tinged with

Keep your veterinarian's number on hand for emergency care.

blood), lethargy, refusal to eat, and fever. (The cause may also be coronavirus, which is not as serious.) While the disease cannot be combated directly, immediate veterinary attention is imperative to provide the supportive fluid therapy required to enable the patient's own body to remain properly hydrated and fight off the infection. Hospitalization, therefore, is vital if this disease's victim is to survive, which can be touch and go depending on the dog's age and overall health before the illness strikes.

Although most dogs are protected from this disease by their annual vaccinations, it is not unusual for even a vaccinated dog to become infected. You might increase your pet's chances of avoiding parvovirus by keeping a puppy somewhat isolated from other dogs or areas that may be vectors of the disease until he has had the full series of vaccinations. Take care to keep your pet's living quarters and kennel or similar areas he frequents clean and disinfected.

Skin Problems

A routine grooming program as well as hands-on examinations of your pet from head to tail are the most effective ways to discover skin problems your dog may be developing. A variety of them exist, caused by everything from flea-bite allergies to bacterial infections to mange, and as is the case with most canine illness, early detection and diagnosis can help ensure that even stubborn skin problems can be conquered with ease.

Lumps, bumps, dryness, incessant scratching, hair loss, and redness are the classic signals that a dog is suffering from skin problems, most of which require a veterinarian's diagnosis to ensure proper treatment. While many conditions may be a challenge to eradicate, some can be prevented through diligent care of the coat and skin, and a sound flea control program.

Urinary Tract Disorders

Dogs are prone to a variety of diseases that can affect the urinary tract, most of them uncomfortable and painful to the dog and many of them quite serious.

Whether caused by a bladder infection, bladder stones, or kidney failure, any sign of urinary tract disease is reason to call the veterinarian. The most vivid signs of a problem here include painful or lack of urination, blood in the urine, a sudden increase in thirst and urination, or any change in urinary habits. Most are fairly evident to the observant owner.

Treatment, of course, depends on cause, which must be determined by a veterinarian who will use such diagnostic tests as urinalysis and blood. Whether it involves medication, surgery, or dietary management, treatment should begin as soon as possible to help prevent the condition from progressing to more dangerous, and possibly deadly, levels, and to relieve the dog's obvious discomfort.

In Case of Emergency

While early diagnosis is key to the successful treatment of most canine ailments, immediate recognition and fast action in some circumstances may be all that stand between survival and death for a dog in an emergency situation. Recognition of acute abdominal pain, for one, should tell an owner that immediate veterinary care is in order, as the cause may be something as critical as bloat or an intestinal obstruction.

Emergency care is most frequently associated with canine injury or similar external causes. An active Alaskan Malamute may be placed in situations where his vigorous lifestyle leads to injuries that may or may not be life threatening, but that in either case require emergency care. A bleeding wound, for example, may require treatment that can't wait for the veterinarian; this dog's survival may rely solely on an owner who knows to apply direct pressure to the wound with a clean cloth to stop the bleeding.

Indeed, life in the great outdoors can hold a variety of emergency threats to this active animal, including snakebite, broken bones, and shock, the latter of which is frequently the result of some other primary catastrophe, such as broken bones or excessive blood loss. Given the fact that many activities in which Mala-

WORDS OF WISDOM

Your pet's first-aid kit can do dual duty as a disaster-preparedness kit. In addition to the first-aid items, outfit the kit with supplies you may need for a quick evacuation or disaster aftermath, and you'll be ready for any earthquake, blizzard, or hurricane that comes your way.

Canine First Aid Kit

The canine first aid kit should contain the following:

✔ a large collection of bandages in various sizes
✔ adhesive tape in one-inch (25 mm) and two-inch (51 mm) widths
✔ cotton dressing pads
✔ rubber gloves
✔ antibiotic ointment
✔ cotton balls and cotton swabs
✔ prescription tranquilizer (some veterinarians recommend Benadryl as an emergency tranquilizer)
✔ saline eyedrops
✔ snakebite kit (available at most camping and large pet supply stores)
✔ diarrhea medicine
✔ first aid how-to manual
✔ hydrogen peroxide
✔ rubbing alcohol (which can also be used to remove tree sap from the coat)
✔ scissors
✔ clean towels
✔ tweezers
✔ petroleum jelly
✔ needle-nose pliers
✔ painkiller (consult your veterinarian for type and dosage)
✔ activated charcoal tablets

Accidents happen, but prevention is the key to keeping your Malamute safe and healthy.

mutes participate are isolated from a neighborhood veterinarian, the owner should prepare ahead of time, both by assembling a well-stocked first aid kit (making sure it is available both at home and away), by learning how to use the items in it, and the various techniques of caring for a dog in specific emergency situations.

One key ingredient in the first aid kit should be a detailed canine first aid guide. While in-depth treatment details for most emergencies extend beyond the scope of this book, having a book handy and familiarizing yourself with its contents will ensure your pet has the best chance of survival should an emergency occur.

If your dog seems a likely candidate for first aid measures because of the lifestyle he shares with you, why not practice ahead of time, too? Learn to apply splints, learn to treat for shock by keeping the dog still and warm, and even learn how to treat snakebites. Your dog will probably view such exercises as a game, but in the long run, that game could save his life.

Poisoning, too, requires fast action; therefore, the savvy owner will remain attuned to the signs of poisoning and, in turn, what potential poisons the dog may have ingested in his environment (such as antifreeze, poisonous plants, or even chocolate). Beyond these obvious measures, be sure to keep the local poison control number on hand. Treatment for some poisons require vomiting, for example, while others absolutely do not, and the poison control personnel are the best resources for determining how to combat each type. Should you suspect poisoning, try to find and/or identify the poison in question, which will help ensure that you will receive more accurate instructions from poison control personnel.

As a dog ages, he may require a change in lifestyle, diet, and exercise routine.

Care of an Old Friend

Care for a dog with diligence and love, and the dog will reap the benefits of living a long and healthy life. One of the most delightful stages of the dog's life comes during his older years, when physically he may slow down a bit, but emotionally he enters a phase when the bond between dog and owner takes on a special glow.

With proper care throughout his life, there is no reason that the Alaskan Malamute cannot enjoy a rewarding and active quality of life well into his teens. This is not to say that things won't change a bit. The Malamute that once spent every weekend showing off his skills in agility, leading a dog team through the snow, or jogging five miles (8.1 km) with an owner in triathlon training may have to modify his activities a bit as he ages. Still, exercise must remain paramount in this dog's schedule, for both the dog's and the owner's well-being.

Walks: One of the most productive commitments you can make toward the care of the older dog is to make room each day for a nice, long walk. Daily walks help keep the older dog's (and the younger dog's) mind clear, his aging joints lubricated, his digestive tract stimulated, and his muscles toned. It also helps keep the dog's weight in check, as many older dogs suffer from an increase in pounds that only serves to stress an aging body and internal systems.

Dogs can adjust well to diminishing senses.

Examinations: The veterinarian plays a key role in the care of the older dog, as well. Geriatric exams conducted twice a year, in which the veterinarian checks the dog's urine and blood, can help detect any budding health problems at the earliest opportunity, and see that treatment begins before those problems have a chance to get worse. The doctor may also recommend adjusting the dog's diet to one of fewer calories and less fat, or to one of the prescription diets now available to help control any health problems the animal may be developing related to aging.

Seeing and hearing problems: Other potential changes require even more of an owner's commitment. As he ages, for example, the dog's sight or hearing may diminish, but this does not need to affect your pet's quality of life. Dogs tend to adjust well to these natural changes, assuming that their owners meet the new challenges with patience and understanding.

Refrain from moving the furniture around if your dog is losing his sight, and prepare for the possibility of a dog losing his hearing by teaching him both verbal commands and hand signals during those formative training years. That way you can be assured of communicating with each other throughout the dog's life.

All in all, there are few callings more rewarding than caring for the older dog. Building a strong foundation of health and mutual respect that will ensure a happy life later on is the first step, after which you will experience a special bond as the beloved companion upon whom you have always depended begins to depend more on you. It is a bond even more acute when shared with the Malamute, a dog that at any age exhibits a most legendary devotion to the human species and a special sensitivity to his family pack.

When It's Time to Say Good-bye

One of the saddest inevitabilities with which every devoted dog owner is intimately acquainted is the fact that we are doomed to outlive our canine companions. Hand in hand with this fact comes the difficult challenge not only of saying good-bye, but of having to make the fateful decision of determining just when that time will be.

Although advancements in veterinary medicine have enabled dogs to live longer, more productive lives than ever before, the time inevitably comes when the dog is either too ill or too much in pain to go on. Although making such a decision can be incredibly devastating for the owner, it takes a great deal of courage and compassion to end that animal's suffering. The decision made, the veterinarian can humanely end the dog's life with an injection that simply puts the dog into a deep and peaceful slumber from which he will not awaken.

Whether the dog passes on naturally in his sleep, is euthanized humanely at the end of a long and productive life, or meets a more untimely, unexpected end, the grief of the owner left behind is genuine and something about which he or she should not be ashamed. Yes, there are individuals who scoff at such deep emotions for companion animals, but they are increasingly in the minority and are certainly missing out on one of life's greatest rewards. Dogs are in every sense family members, and it is perfectly legitimate, and even necessary, to grieve for their loss, whether alone, with trusted friends and family members, or even with one of the support groups that specialize in this particular type of grief.

While one's initial response to the loss of a longtime canine companion may be the thought that he or she will never have another dog, those who have been through it know that the enrichment these animals bring to our lives far outweighs any grief that inevitably comes at the end of the relationship. Which brings us to the question of welcoming another dog into the family.

Once a person has lived with an Alaskan Malamute, he or she often finds it quite difficult to live without one. The question is when to bring a new Malamute into the family. For some, the best remedy for healing the broken heart caused by the loss of one dog is to bring another into the home as soon as possible. For others, a period of mourning must occur before

Keep your Malamute active but comfortable in his senior years.

making the commitment again. Either way, when that new dog joins the family, you must not expect the new addition to be a clone of the one who came before. Each is an individual with his own special brand of Malamute joy to bring to your home. Love and cherish this dog for who he is, just as you loved and cherished his predecessor.

A COMMITMENT TO ACTIVITY

Exercise for a Malamute—or for any dog—does far more than simply work the dog's muscles, bones, and joints. The benefits of a solid exercise regimen are limitless in scope.

Body and Soul

Bringing an Alaskan Malamute into your home means providing that dog with daily activity through which she may expend her abundant energies. No, you need not harness the dog to a sled for a rollicking jaunt through the snow—although your pet will be most pleased if you do so—but she must be entertained with plenty of exercise that will do you both good.

Yes, physical activity does keep a dog fit and probably living longer than she would if she were relegated to life as a couch potato. Yes, it helps prevent obesity, a condition epidemic in America's canine population today, and yes, it improves a dog's circulation and digestion. But an added bonus that many owners may

Life with an Alaskan Malamute means never forgetting the dog's long history as working dog and athlete.

not think of is the fact that when a dog gets out into the world, her mind as well as body are stimulated by the experience, and the dog will end up being a better pet.

A dog that is accustomed to daily activity and interaction with the wonderful scents, sights, and sensations beyond the boundaries of her home turf is far less likely to become a victim of separation anxiety and a practitioner of home demolition and incessant barking. The dog is fulfilled body and soul and therefore has no reason to protest.

Do not think, however, that simply turning this dog out into your backyard will garner such benefits. There is no lazy way out of living with a Malamute. This is a partnership to which both partners must commit. That commitment is second nature to the Malamute, evident in the leaps of joy you will encounter every time she spots the leash in your hand, even if torrents of rain are falling outside or the weather

=========== T I P ===========

Rules of the Trail

When you hike or mush into the wilderness with your Malamute, it is important to respect Mother Nature. Abide by her following rules, and she may just let you come back sometime.

✔ Pack out what you pack in (food leftovers, garbage, etc.).

✔ Keep your dog on leash at all times and don't allow her to harass or chase wildlife.

✔ Keep all fires under control for the safety of the wilderness, yourself, and your dog.

✔ Store food properly to avoid inviting the attentions of resident wildlife.

✔ Enjoy....

report just informed you that it's 20-below with the wind chill.

Needless to say, the commitment may not come so easily to the human partner, who may at times be tempted to forget that the Malamute's high activity level was a characteristic that drew him or her to this breed in the first place. One way to deal with this is not to dread the time you must devote each day to acting as your Malamute's personal trainer, but to see it as natural to your day as eating or breathing. Your dog will certainly view it this way. Join her in her wisdom.

Health Considerations

Ideally, your Malamute should have her first introductions to physical activity as a young puppy. Her exuberant puppy antics, attacking

tennis shoes, rolling under the coffee table, speeding through the halls after the kids, and puppy kindergarten fun, combined with restful naps and quiet times, will usher the youngster in to what awaits her as an adult. But, though the Malamute is a natural athlete of legendary strength and endurance, you must not ignore common sense in preparing her for physical activity. Consider the demands such activities will place on the dog, and prepare the animal accordingly.

If the dog has been relatively sedentary of late, perhaps receiving two half-hour walks a day, but you would like to venture into recreational mushing, skijoring, agility, or even jogging with your pet, she must be introduced to the new vocation gradually so as not to overly tax her system or strain muscles. This will also give you time to introduce your pet to any special equipment that may be required, such as a harness or a different type of lead. Most Malamutes, excited by the prospect of a new adventure and driven by their compulsion to work with and please their owners, won't hold back when asked to work, regardless of their physical condition, so it's the owners' job to ensure they proceed safely.

The best bet is first to have the dog examined by the veterinarian to ensure she is up to the new tasks. The doctor can inspect the dog's legs, heart, lungs, and feet, and together you can discuss her diet as well as design a safe conditioning program. For jogging, this may simply mean keeping the dog on her usual maintenance diet, enticing her to drink a bit more water, and starting her out running short distances that gradually lengthen every few days. For a newcomer to mushing, however, the doctor may prescribe a high-energy diet or nutritional supplements, as well as training exercises, in which the dog first pulls a wheeled cart along a clean, snow-free road before tackling winter conditions.

You must also consider the climate. For obvious reasons, most Malamutes work best in cooler, preferably cold, temperatures. It's the heat you need to worry about. During summer, therefore, restrict vigorous activity to the cooler times of the morning and evening. Make sure the dog is not exposed to direct sunlight or her feet subjected to hot pavement, and watch her carefully for heavy or shallow breathing, pale gums, profuse salivation, or a wobbly gait that could indicate heatstroke. And regardless of the weather, hot or cold, make sure the dog drinks plenty of fresh, clean water throughout the day. You certainly don't want your efforts to satisfy your dog's energy needs to be tainted by unnecessary tragedy.

Activities Within the Family

Although the Malamute will revel in the opportunity to work as a sled dog, this is not the only game in town for this breed. Malamutes excel in a variety of activities, most of which begin at home.

Daily walks: A family of committed Malamute owners can provide their pet with plenty of mental and physical stimulation without ever setting foot in the arctic. While the suburban neighborhood may seem old hat to you, each day offers a whole new treasure trove of exciting, as-yet-to-be-discovered sights, smells, and experiences to your dog.

You can thrust your dog into the midst of this homespun adventure simply by taking her out on walks twice a day, preferably with the whole family in tow. Because the Malamute is a sled dog by breeding, she may be inclined to pull ahead. To remedy this, some owners have come to prefer an H-shape harness or a head halter to the more traditional neck collars. Used correctly, the halter in particular, along with some training in this area, can help temper the dog's impulse to pull.

Hiking: If you would like to carry walking a step further, try hiking with your pet, another natural occupation for this dog that is content to follow her owner anywhere—especially if there is snow on the ground. Begin with half-day hikes, and work up to the whole day once you're both up to it. So inspired, you may even want to try an overnight backpacking trip. A well-trained Malamute will gladly carry her own pack, which she may want to do on your shorter walks, as well.

Regardless of whether you are walking for half a day or a weekend, bring along ample supplies for the dog, including healthy treats and food, water, bedding, and a first aid kit. Remember, too, to abide by all rules to ensure that the trails remain open to dogs in the future.

Hot wheels: Because of her size, talents, and conformation, the Malamute is somewhat grounded in what she can do in the way of exercise. You, on the other hand, are not. Yet even when you are participating in an activity that takes you above the ground on a set of wheels, your Malamute may still join you as an active and willing participant.

The most popular of such activities are bicycling and roller skating (either with in-line skates or the old fashioned four-wheel variety). Once you decide that you would like to teach your dog to lope alongside you as you ride a

Sled Dog Commands

The following are music to a sled dog's ears. They are the commands that Malamutes who are trained to pull a sled know and love, because they represent the work these dogs were born to do. (By the way, you won't find "mush" on the list, a command you will surely hear in movies, but never from the mouths of genuine "mushers.")

- Gee: go right
- Haw: go left
- Hike: let's go
- Straight on: keep going straight, don't turn
- Pick it up: increase the speed
- Whoa: stop

bike or skate, don't for a minute forget that the partner you are inviting along is a sled dog in mind and heart. In other words, she harbors an inner and almost uncontrollable desire to pull. If not properly trained to accompany a cyclist or skater, the results when those innate pulling instincts kick in can be devastating to the party on wheels at the other end of the leash.

Train your dog to join you in these pursuits in much the same way you teach her other skills. Make each experience as positive as it can be, which should be a breeze considering that the Malamute is a perfect candidate to accompany you on these forays.

Start with the fundamentals. Work first in perfecting your dog's skills on leash, perhaps with a halter or H-shape harness, convincing this big powerful dog that pulling on the leash

really isn't what she should be doing. Work on this until you trust the dog implicitly not to pull while you are walking or running, then try it on wheels. Build up distances gradually, a benefit both to the dog's health and to helping her adjust to the new sensation of running alongside someone on skates or a bicycle.

Think of your own safety, too. Wear a helmet if you are cycling with a Malamute by your side; add knee pads and elbow pads if you are bringing your dog along while you skate. You never know when a sudden impulse, scent, or sound will capture your pet's imagination. Should this occur, you'll be thankful you took the time to outfit yourself with safety gear that can prevent the type of serious injuries that can only happen when one is on wheels and being pulled by a large dog.

Snow and Cold: The Malamute's Calling

While a Malamute can enjoy any number of activities, her heart is where the snow is. Take an adult Malamute who has never seen snow up to the mountains in winter for an introduction. The blanket of white and the cold rustling through her coat will instantly trigger an ancient preprogrammed passion in the dog and summon those ancient memories. This is home. You may never convince your dog to leave.

The truly fortunate Malamute belongs to people whose motivation for obtaining such a dog was to spend time with her in the snow, whether or not they happen to live in snow country. Make the effort, and your Malamute will be eternally grateful.

Mushing: The sport of mushing has enjoyed burgeoning popularity in the past few years.

The Alaskan Malamute is a large active dog that requires an owner who is equally dedicated to activity.

While such annual races as the Iditarod and the Yukon Quest attract more interest each year, and mushers dream of seeing sled dog racing become an Olympic sport, even those who aren't up to entering the legendary 1,000-plus-mile (1,610-plus-km) endurance races can enjoy this sport on a recreational basis.

The beauty of mushing with a Malamute is that, because this dog is a freighting dog rather than a classic racer, you only need one or two dogs to make a team. Participation does require some preparation, of course, both in training and in procuring the right equipment. You will need a sled, and you will need proper harnessing, which are available from specialty supply houses, online, through mail order, and from manufacturers typically located in regions where sledding is popular. Ideally, you will also need snow, but you can get by harnessing the dog to a wheeled cart, which is actually a good way to condition and train the dog when there is no snow available.

Before you get started, however, attend some mushing events and visit the mushers you meet there. The benefit of the sport's increasing popularity is that you are now more likely to find such events advertised in local newspapers. If not, contact your local kennel club as well as the national breed clubs for the sledding breeds. These sources should be able to point you in the right direction, and they may also be able to recommend trainers in your area who instruct beginners on the sport of mushing.

Given that mushing is not the ideal sport for do-it-yourself training, learning hands-on from

the experts is the smartest and safest way to go. Most newcomers are astounded at the terrific power that emanates from sled dogs as they revel in the role for which they were bred and born. That power can be dangerous in the hands of an untrained novice, so get the training you and your dog need, from handling the sled to the proper commands, and enjoy.

Though pulling a sled is a natural calling to the Alaskan Malamute, this is only one of the many activities open to these dogs and their owners.

Skijoring: If you find the idea of mushing a dog team through the snow a bit too intimidating, there is an alternative: skijoring. In a more exciting, fast-action version of cross-country skiing, instead of a sled, you are on skis and the dog does what she loves most—she pulls you through the snow.

Although skijoring sounds simpler than classic mushing, it can be dangerous, so it is wise to get formal training, and while skijoring is more accessible to most people than mushing, it can also be more of a challenge as it is just you and the dog—no sled as a buffer.

To master the skill of skijoring, you should first master the art of standing up and getting around on skis; otherwise, the dog lurches forward, you fall over, and the rest becomes a very painful, cold memory. At the same time, work with the dog without skis, polishing up the obedience commands and mimicking skijoring by running with your dog (preferably in the snow). Expand your pet's vocabulary by working on turning and stopping commands, which will be vital out on the trail.

Soon you will be entrusting your well-being to your dog, so you must be able to trust and control this powerful animal. For your first outing—preferably with your instructor—choose a relatively quiet, familiar, flat area, free of distractions and overly challenging trails. Build up the time you spend at it gradually, and remember not to skimp on the harnessing. Whether mushing a team of dogs from a sled or sharing a singular skijoring excursion with your beloved pet, proper harnessing can make the experience more pleasant—and safe—for you both.

The Show Spotlight

Formal showing is a unique avenue open to those who seek to get involved in what is known as the sport of dogs. In addition to providing a showcase for dogs, dog shows also offer a convenient opportunity for would-be Malamute owners to meet breeders and their dogs in a single location. Even if you choose not to show your dog, the shows can be paradise for those who revel in the company of purebred Malamutes.

Conformation Showing

Often referred to as beauty pageants for dogs, conformation shows, in which dogs are judged for appearance and movement as they are trotted around a ring by a handler, represent far more than simply a venue for owners to show off their pets. The purpose of the conformation show is to foster the breeding of dogs that meet their breed standards; the working breeds are judged on how well they embody the structure required for the jobs they have long been bred for.

Yes, the dogs in the conformation show ring are beautifully turned out, well groomed, obedient, and attentive, but because the champion Malamute's legs and shoulders are of the correct angles, because her coat is of just the right texture and density, because her bite is perfectly aligned, and because her back is not too short or too long, this dog, theoretically, would also be ideally engineered for work in the snow. Of course, it doesn't always happen that way—most show dogs never even participate in the vocations for which they were bred—but the theory is sound.

At AKC dog shows, registered Malamutes compete in the Working Group. The entrants are pitted first against other Malamutes, the winners ultimately making their way through several rungs until the Best of Breed is determined. The Best of Breed winner then competes against all the other Working Group Best of Breed winners for the Best of Group title. Within this competition the dogs are to be judged not against each other, but on how well each exemplifies its individual standard. Should the Malamute be chosen best of the Working Group, she then moves on to compete for the coveted title of Best in Show.

The ideal show dog is the dog who stands as a shining example of her breed's standard, but who also truly enjoys prancing around that ring. In addition to physique and movement, judges look for a sparkle in the eye, a special inner thrill at being on stage. Some dogs just simply seem to be born to it.

Needless to say, not every Malamute is cut out for the show ring. If showing is something that might interest you, think about that before you choose a puppy and work with a reputable breeder. He or she will guide you toward the show-quality puppies in a given litter, and, ideally, work with you to help foster your puppy's show talents. Keep in mind, however, that this does not mean the pet-quality Malamutes in that litter are any less valuable. They, too, have reaped the benefits of the careful breeding that produces fine show prospects and are destined to make, just as their name implies, the finest of pets. Their callings just happen to lie in directions other than that of the conformation show ring.

Obedience Trials

One of the callings that may be of interest to a Malamute owner is obedience competition. Be warned, however, that because of this dog's independent spirit and strong-willed ideas about what she will and will not do, the Malamute's is not a face one commonly sees in the winner's circle at obedience trials. Yet there are dedicated owners who have set the earning of obedience titles as goals for their dogs, and they have succeeded.

At obedience trials, which are typically held in conjunction with conformation shows and are usually sanctioned by either the American Kennel Club or the United Kennel Club, dogs exhibit their ability to obey specific commands. The demands on the dogs grow increasingly challenging depending on the level of the titles for which they are competing.

Obedience offers all dogs an opportunity to shine regardless of their fitness as conformation show competitors, and it provides the ideal outlet for dogs and owners to work together as a team toward a common goal. While the canine component of the team usually understands that goal and is thrilled to participate, stories abound of Malamutes that have worked diligently for months, and then, when it's time for the real test, choose to exercise the legendary Malamute sense of humor and conveniently forget all that they have been taught. The main ingredient, then, for the owner who chooses to compete with a Malamute in obedience is a sense of humor equal to that of the dog's.

Activities for Every Malamute

Organized events in which dogs, all dogs, can participate abound. This comes as good news for people who would like to be involved in such activities with their dogs, but thought that conformation showing was the only option.

The weight pull: One such option open to Malamutes is weight pulling. While Siberian huskies and Alaskan huskies are considered the quintessential racing dogs, Malamutes occupy their own unique niche as kings of the weight pullers.

On its surface—and in the works of Jack London—weight pulling may appear somewhat cruel, but weight pulling is actually a very civilized activity (more so than it was during the rush for Yukon gold), and the dogs trained to participate, including Malamutes, relish the opportunity to make their owners proud. The International Weight Pull Association sponsors weight pulls in which dogs of various breeds

and mixes of breeds compete in appropriate weight categories, pulling either sleds or wheeled carts for specified distances in prescribed time limits.

This activity obviously requires a commitment from the owner to the dog's training and conditioning, time spent that simultaneously fosters a unique and historical bond between the two. The dog is initially introduced to the special weight-training harness and the sensation of pulling very light weights. As the animal's strength and inclination develop, with the help of daily workouts and an athlete's diet, the weight is gradually increased. Once the load is too heavy for the dog, she will typically sit or stand still, the universal signal that she has finished for the day.

Attend an organized weight pull, and you will witness the beauty of a unique bond that can exist between a human being and a dog. Watch the dogs as they strive to please the people they call their own, and listen to those people as they encourage their dogs, speaking softly to them in a language that only they share.

Agility: Agility events are often held in conjunction with more traditional conformation shows, and you are likely to find quite a large gathering of spectators congregating to witness these exciting events. Both agility training and the events themselves offer dog owners fun alternatives to more formal dog showing, and there is no better way to keep both dog and owner healthy, active, and young at heart.

When competing in this activity, the dog, with the coaching of her owner, makes her way through a canine obstacle course designed to showcase the dog's agility. Running, jumping, traversing, bobbing, and weaving, she attempts to complete the course quickly and with as few faults as possible, all to the enthusiastic cheers of the crowd. Needless to say, mastering agility skills requires training and conditioning, but the fun element is supreme. Win or lose, agility is a delightful event that, not surprisingly, is increasing in popularity each year.

Canine Good Citizen: Finally, when considering formal activities that you and your dog can pursue together, don't forget the American Kennel Club's Canine Good Citizen test. The CGC is a special title any dog can earn that proves to the world that this animal is the ideal canine companion.

To earn those coveted initials, the dog must pass several tests, which may require a bit of training ahead of time. The dog seeking this high accolade for her good citizenship must exhibit her mastery of basic obedience commands; she must permit a stranger to pet, touch, and brush her; she must walk on a leash without pulling (fortunately for the Malamute, she need not do this at the heel); and she must show that she can ignore visual and sound distractions.

Agility is a fun activity in which Malamutes of all ages and abilities can participate.

This is not a simple test for all dogs to pass, but those letters "CGC" after a dog's name are indeed something of which both dog and owner may be eternally proud. As an added bonus, once earned, the CGC opens an infinite number of doors to a dog, for the better citizen a dog is, the more welcome she will be wherever she may roam.

Organizations

The Alaskan Malamute Club of America
Leneia Rogowski, Corresponding Secretary
640 E. 50 N
Hyrum, UT 84319-1454
www.alaskanmalamute.org

Alaskan Malamute Assistance League
www.malamuterescue.org
Offers Malamute rescue information and provides contact names of rescuers nationwide.

The American Kennel Club
260 Madison Avenue
New York, NY 10016
(212) 696-8200
www.akc.org

The Canadian Kennel Club
89 Skyway Avenue, Suite 100
Etobicoke, Ontario, Canada M9W 6R4
(416) 675-5511
www.ckc.ca

The Minnesota Malamute Club
www.minnesotamalamuteclub.com
Dedicated to both the well-being of Alaskan Malamutes and the preservation of the breed's working traditions.

Health Organizations

The Orthopedic Foundation for Animals
2300 E. Nifong Boulevard
Columbia, MO 65201
(573) 442-0418
www.offa.org

The AMCA Chondrodysplasia Certification Committee
www.alaskanmalamute.org/Health/chd/chd.asp

www.malamutehealth.org
Excellent resource for issues related to the health of Alaskan Malamutes

Periodicals

The Alaskan Malamute Club of America Newsletter
c/o AMCA Corresponding Secretary
640 E 50 N
Hyrum, UT 84319
www.alaskanmalamute.org

The American Kennel Club Gazette
260 Madison Avenue
New York, NY 10016
(212) 696-8200
www.akc.org

Dog Fancy Magazine
Dog World Magazine
P.O. Box 6050
Mission Viejo, CA 92690
www.dogchannel.com

Mushing Magazine
3875 Geist Road, Suite 246
Fairbanks, AK 99709-3549
(917) 929-6118
www.mushing.com

From puppyhood on, participation in a variety of activities with her owners will strengthen the dog/family bond.

Books

Baer, Ted, *Communicating with Your Dog*, 2nd edition, Barron's Educational Series, Inc., Hauppauge, NY, 1999.

Campbell, William, *Behavior Problems in Dogs*, Dogwise Publishing, Wenatchee, WA, 1999.

Dunbar, Ian, *Before and After Getting Your Puppy: The Positive Approach to Raising a Happy, Healthy, and Well-Behaved Dog*, New World Library, Novato, CA, 2004.

Fogle, Bruce, D.V.M., *First Aid for Dogs: What to do When Emergencies Happen*, Penguin, New York, NY, 1997.

Giffin, James M., M.D., and Carlson, Liisa D., D.V.M., *Dog Owner's Home Veterinary Handbook*, Howell Reference Books, New York, NY, 1999.

Riddle, Maxwell, and Harris, Beth J., *The New Complete Alaskan Malamute*, Howell Book House, New York, NY, 1990.

Wrede, Barbara, *Civilizing Your Puppy*, 2nd edition, Barron's Educational Series, Inc., Hauppauge, NY, 1997.

About the Author

Betsy Sikora Siino is an award-winning writer of more than 25 books and hundreds of articles, primarily on subjects related to animals and their care. As a former staff writer for such publications as *Dog Fancy, Dogs USA, Pet Health News,* and *Horse Illustrated* magazines, she has a special affinity for horses, wildlife, and, most of all, dogs, particularly for the great northern breeds (the Alaskan Malamute, the Samoyed, and the Siberian Husky among them). A graduate of the University of California at Davis, Betsy is a member of the Author's Guild and the Dog Writers Association of America, from which she has received award recognition for her work on wolf/dog hybrids and wild canids. She has a special interest in subjects related to wild species and has received acclaim for her work on wolves, coyotes, and other large predators.

Important Note

This pet owner's guide tells the reader how to buy and care for an Alaskan Malamute. The author and the publisher consider it important to point out that the advice given in the book is meant primarily for normally developed puppies from a good breeder—that is, dogs of excellent physical health and good character.

Anyone who adopts a fully grown dog should be aware that the animal has already formed its basic impressions of human beings. The new owner should watch the animal carefully, including its behavior toward humans, and should meet the previous owner. If the dog comes from a shelter, it may be possible to get some information on the dog's background and peculiarities there. There are dogs that, as a result of bad experiences with humans, behave in an unnatural manner or may even bite. Only people that have experience with dogs should take in such animals.

Caution is further advised in the association of children with dogs, in meeting with other dogs, and in exercising the dog without a leash.

Even well-behaved and carefully supervised dogs sometimes do damage to someone else's property or cause accidents. It is therefore in the owner's interest to be adequately insured against such eventualities, and we strongly urge all dog owners to purchase a liability policy that covers their dog.

Photo Credits

Cheryl Ertelt: pages 2–3, 4, 11, 15, 24, 25, 34, 35, 46, 54, 59, 66, 79, 81, 91; Isabelle Francais: pages 13, 19, 27, 30, 39, 41, 48, 51, 56, 60, 63, 67, 68, 70, 87, 93; Kent Dannen: pages 16, 29, 37, 42, 47, 62, 76, 88; Susan Green: pages 9, 61; Michael Siino: pages 6, 22, 75; Tara Darling: pages 5, 83; Bob Schwartz: pages 57, 74, 80; Karen Hudson: pages 12, 33, 82; Bonnie Nance: page 73.

Cover Photos

Front cover: Isabelle Francais; Back cover: Pets by Paulette; Inside front cover: Kent Dannen; Inside back cover: Karen Hudson.

All inquiries should be addressed to:
Barron's Educational Series, Inc.
250 Wireless Boulevard
Hauppauge, NY 11788
www.barronseduc.com

ISBN-13: 978-0-7641-3676-4
ISBN-10: 0-7641-3676-3

Library of Congress Catalog Card No. 2007018998

Library of Congress Cataloging-in-Publication Data
Siino, Betsy Sikora.
    Alaskan malamutes : everything about purchase, care, nutrition, behavior, and training : with full-color photographs / Betsy Sikora Siino ; illustrations by Tana Hakanson.
        p. cm.
        ISBN-13: 978-0-7641-3676-4 (alk. paper)
        ISBN-10: 0-7641-3676-3 (alk. paper)
        1. Alaskan Malamute. I. Title.

SF429.A67S55   2007
636.73—dc22   2007018998

Printed in China
9 8 7 6